THE COMPLETE MOTORCYCLE NOMAD

THE COMPLETE MOTORCYCLE NOMAD

A GUIDE TO MACHINES, EQUIPMENT, PEOPLE, AND PLACES

ROGER LOVIN

Illustrated by the Author
A Sports Illustrated Book
Little, Brown and Company • Boston • Toronto

FIRST EDITION

T02/74

Sports Illustrated Books
are published by
Little, Brown and Company
in association with
Sports Illustrated Magazine

Library of Congress Cataloging in Publication Data

Lovin, Roger.
The complete motorcycle nomad.

Bibliography: p.
1. Motorcycling. I. Title.
GV1059.5.L68 1974 796.7'5 73-17057
ISBN 0-316-53355-6
ISBN 0-316-53356-4 (pbk.)

Published simultaneously in Canada
By Little, Brown & Company (Canada) Limited

PRINTED IN THE UNITED STATES OF AMERICA

For Goyathlay, whom the Mexicans called Geronimo.
He wasn't much for fences.

This book is about motorcycles and highways and cities, about how they interact, and about how you can use them to get from here to there successfully.

CONTENTS

PART THREE: CITIES

THE COMPLETE MOTORCYCLE NOMAD

KÖLN
15
KM

INTRODUCTION: 1,160 WORDS ON MOTORCYCLES, NOMADS, AND THIS BOOK

We owe the existence of the motorcycle to Gottlieb Daimler, who built the first one in 1885 in a greenhouse in Cannstatt, Germany. What a monster it was! It had a 264 cc engine mounted on a velocipede, with iron-shod wooden wheels fore and aft and training wheels to either side. It weighed 198 pounds, carried a single passenger, and was capable of nearly 7½ mph, provided the road was flat.

But however crude, it *was* a motorcycle, and from it sprang all the two-wheelers that populate the highways today.

If we owe the motorcycle to Gottlieb, we owe its popularity, in this country at least, to Japan's remarkable Mr. Honda. His line of low-priced and reliable machines opened up the world of motorcycling to a whole generation of Americans and paved the way for Japan's Revenge — the import explosion of the 1960s.

Before Honda, motorcycling in the United States was the province of the outcast, the hairy-chested, and the fanatic. With the introduction of Honda's light- and medium-weight bikes, and with the flood of competitors that followed him, motorcycling became a respectable, if somewhat precarious, pursuit.

Today, with nearly five million bikes in this country, motorcycling is a valid part of the American experience. Little brother tears up the yard with his minibike, Sis rides a 175 cc to school, Dad rides a dirt bike, pretending he's Genghis Khan, and Granny has swapped her pool cue for a moto-cross machine and is registered for this year's Elsinore run.

And you? Well, maybe you want to run out to the coast for the summer.

Daimler gave motorcycles to the world, and Honda gave them to America. But who gave us our urge to throw frying pan and bedroll on them and go off over the horizon? It is a fact that Americans are the most nomadic people in history. We travel more and farther, for more diverse reasons, than the people of any other nation in the world. It is estimated that one in four Americans spends some part of each year away from home. The average American — average, mind you — changes his address once every five years.

We are nomads, then, and with a vengeance.

None of which explains why so many people ride off on a bike amid the forty-ton semis and rush-hour maniacs.

Personally, I believe it is combination of factors involving both the inherent character of motorcycles and a loose screw in our national psyche.

Motorcycles are freedom symbols. They are not subject to the strictures of today's group-goal, success-oriented world. Motorcycling is a solitary venture, potentially dangerous, that requires of the practitioner a whole range of highly specialized skills. Bikes place a person in immediate contact with the environment, giving him full benefit of the wind and sun — and rain and cold and bugs. Motorcycles are, in short, exhilarating machines, capable of producing the odd moment of sheer ecstasy in their riders, and this is an emotion in which our times are sadly deficient.

The loose screw I mentioned involves our persistent refusal to admit that the buffalo are gone from the range — or, for that matter, that the range itself is long vanished. Though our eyes see only herds of Chevrolets and Volkswagens grazing peacefully beneath the towering Howard Johnsons, deep in all our hearts we *know* that Kit Carson and Geronimo are still out there, if only we can find them.

Furthermore, we all know that we are at least as capable of surviving in the wastelands as Tarzan, and yearn for the opportunity to prove it. Which is utter nonsense, of course. But nonsense of such power that each year some twenty or thirty million of us pack up and go looking for it. Of this number, close to a million and a half of us do it on motorcycles. Including me.

I have a BMW R68 so old that by the time you read this, he will be legally an antique. I have named him Ganesh, after the elephant-headed Hindu diety, because his long suit is strength and dependability. He had a quarter-million miles on him when I found him, and I have doubled that figure since then. In all those miles and years, he has cost me less than $200 in repairs.

Ganesh and I have traveled most of the United States, some of Canada, and a good part of Mexico and Central America. My relationship with Ganesh is personal; I consider him a friend. We are in our sixth year of traveling now and anticipate many more.

Not all nomads "personalize" their machines, but most do. There is a symbiosis set up between man and machine in any form of travel, for travel is less forgiving of mistakes than sedentary life. You depend on your machine to function safely, and it depends on you for care and maintenance. This is precisely the same relationship the Bedouin has with his camel, the Apache with his pony, the Eskimo with his dogs, and the Gypsy with his horse. The fact that the relationship is human/animal in one case and human/machine in the other has no significance: it is a symbiosis in both instances. If the Bedouin does not tend his camel's feet, it will quit on him in the desert. If the biker does not tend his mount's "feet," it will quit on him on the freeway — usually at about 65 mph.

There is one difference between the classic nomads of history and today's two-wheel traveler, though. Each of the nomadic cultures had a body of experience to fall back on. The Bedouin had a hundred generations of desert lore behind him when first he mounted his camel. The Eskimo had a codified set of oral rules for traveling the ice. The Apache could usually ride a pony before he could walk.

But for the motorcycle nomad, there is no vast body of gathered wisdom. True, there have been long-distance bikers for as long as there have been motorcycles, but they have left no literature behind. And they numbered in the thousands, at best. Today motorcyclists number in the millions, and we are still without a literature.

We are also without supportive technology. There are no tents designed specifically for bike use, no cook kits made just for the motorcyclist, no storage systems designed for the two-wheel nomad.

Consequently, the biker must modify equipment meant for other uses; must invent solutions to problems long since solved for the automobile tourer; must, to an extent rare in today's world, be self-sufficient and self-reliant.

Which, after all, is what it's all about.

The successful nomad is the practical nomad, for travel is adventure and adventure is a practical business. His rules are more stringent than those of the nontraveler, and the consequences of flouting them more serious. If a person makes a bad choice in armchairs, he will suffer, at most, discomfort. If he makes a bad choice in motorcycles, however . . .

It is my purpose in this book to help the potential bike nomad avoid the fatal mistakes. To do this, I have taken the premise that bike touring can be regarded as a system and the system can be reduced to component parts, among which are the motorcycle, the equipment it carries, the highways it passes over, the cities it passes through, and the knowledge and attitudes of the rider. These components, and the way they interact with one another, form a complete mental and physical environment with the nomad himself at the center.

It's an egocentric view, but it works.

The mode of the book is quite simple. I have assumed complete innocence on your part, and omnipotence on mine. With every aspect of bike nomadics, from clothing yourself properly to dealing with fear and loathing in a strange town, I show you how *I* do it.

Just to keep my ego in check, I also give you the opinions and experiences of other nomads whenever applicable and attempt to present as wide a range of philosophies on the subject in question as possible. However, final opinions are mine unless I state otherwise, simply because I have tested everything I advocate myself and know firsthand that it works.

The book is divided into three sections: "Motorcycles," "Highways," and "Cities."

"Motorcycles" takes you through the whole process of outfitting yourself with a compact "home" and selecting a bike to carry it on.

"Highways" covers riding and camping techniques, survival on the trackless interstate system, and the care and feeding of your equipment.

"Cities" deals with people-concentrates, with life in the oasis, and with how to speak your native language.

At the back of the book is a short chapter on nomadism per se, in which we consider why anyone in his right mind would live in Los Angeles when he could be living on a motorcycle.

And tucked away at the very back of the book is a Sources Appendix, which shows you where to find further information on various subjects, where to purchase specific equipage, and what to expect in prices.

But first things first. Let's get you mounted.

New Orleans
March 30, 1973

PART I: MOTORCYCLES

A motorcycle is . . .

A mechanical horse.
A work of the devil.
Freedom.
A good way to get killed.
A sex substitute.
The most absurd form of transportation yet devised.

I.

CHOOSING YOUR MOUNT

Selecting the proper motorcycle to put under you is an important decision. Your mount will be the foundation of your traveling home, the chair you sit on all day, the force that moves you over the horizon. It will be tool, friend, and extension of yourself; a complex device on which you must depend in critical situations.

Traditionally, the two-wheel nomad's mount is a big, powerful touring bike like the BMW or the Harley-Davidson. But I have known people who have gone around the world happily and comfortably on Honda Cubs. I once met a couple from Pakistan who had covered most of Europe and Asia on a Lambretta scooter with a sidecar.

So your first move in picking a mount is to drop your preconceptions. Realize that a touring bike is any bike that will carry you and your gear over the roads you want to travel at the speeds you wish to go.

The Three-Vector System

Note the three factors given above: speed, carrying capacity, and terrain. These things will determine the type and, to an extent, size bike that best fits you. They are intertwined and can be expressed as a three-vector system.

Look at each potential mount from the three viewpoints of its weight-carrying capacity, its cruising speed with a load, and its suitability to the kinds of roads you want to travel. Choose your mount from the bikes whose capabilities all "vector" together within your requirement limits.

For example, if your "house" is pretty heavy, and you like to get down the freeway at a rapid pace, you will need a big road bike, a true tourer. But if you travel with just a toothbrush and a frying pan, you could get away with a medium-sized street bike or even one of the on-road/off-road machines, like a Hodaka Wombat. Again, maybe you and your gear run to a lot of weight, but you like to putt down the back roads at 45 mph. At those slow speeds you could get away with that Honda Cub I mentioned (I once met a nurse from Sydney, Australia, who was into her forty-thousandth mile of round-the-world nomadics, carrying on a 50 cc Honda more gear than I had on Ganesh.)

Think your requirements out carefully. Make an accurate estimate of the weight you are going to ask your mount to bear, the kinds of roads you are going to utilize, and the swiftness of your traveling. Establish the parameters of each factor: weight from so much to so much, roads from this kind to that kind, cruising between thus and so speeds. Consider compromising on one or more factors. Do you really need to cruise at 70? If so, can you sacrifice some weight without cramping yourself? How much time will you actually spend crossing deserts?

The rule is: the wider your parameters, the wider your selection of potential mounts.

The three-vector system will give you a rough idea of the size and type of bike that will fit your needs. To get more specific you must examine each of the many factors that determine a given bike's suitability for nomadics. Let's look at them one at a time.

Weight

Weight is the most critical factor in a nomad's mount. All of a bike's handling and performance characteristics are affected by the amount and distribution of the weight it carries. An overloaded mount will handle badly in turns, lose up to 65 percent of its braking ability, and suffer serious losses in acceleration. Its cruising stability will be impaired, making it a chore to ride and unsafe in high-wind situations. Riding an overloaded bike in the rain will produce many interesting stories to tell later, if there is a later.

Overloading a bike does two bad things. It changes the center of gravity of the bike, and it strains the power plant. The handling and stability of a motorcycle depend largely on where its center of gravity is located. The closer to the ground that center of gravity is, the more stable the ride. When you overload your machine you raise the center of gravity, sometimes radically. This results in side stress on the suspension components, extra work on the rider's part, and sometimes frame oscillation, which is a fore-and-aft figure-eight motion through the frame, about which there is nothing good to say.

Loading your mount beyond its power capacities is one of the quickest ways to attract trouble. Power transfers from the engine to the rear wheel, and stress transfers from the rear wheel back through the engine. This means that the entire system — chain, transmission, engine — is affected by any overload. Stress on one part will reflect itself through all other parts. When the engine suffers, so do the transmission and chain. For that matter, so do the clutch, the shocks, the tires, etc. Every bearing in your bike, from the transmission to the steering races, will bide its time until it catches you in a blizzard in Vermont, then go on strike. Aside from the impossibility of enjoying yourself while waiting nervously for something to give up, consider that the piece that breaks first in an overloaded machine will probably be something internal. Tire-patch kits are available most anywhere, but main bearings aren't.

How do you determine a given motorcycle's load capacity? Read the specifications. Bear in mind, though, that what the specs give you is usually an ultimate, not an average. If the manufacturer rates a bike at 250 pounds carrying capacity, it will carry that, but not for a long time, no more than it will run at full throttle indefinitely. You have to give yourself a weight leeway the same as you do a power leeway. Roughly, choose a bike with 20 percent more load rating than you intend to put on it. Remember that load distribution will have more effect on your mount's handling than total weight. (Proper loading is covered in Chapter Eleven.) The goal to aim for is a bike that is 25 percent heavier than the load it will carry. Finally, remember that an overloaded bike is an overworked bike, and that it will tell you so sooner or later.

Stability

Stability is a desirable characteristic in any motorcycle, and a necessary one in a nomad's mount. Running all day on a bike you have to fight is dangerous. Fatigue becomes a real threat, blurring your judgment and inviting sudden changes of status. Stability is achieved by correctness of design and correctness of usage. You, the rider, have no control over the former except through your purchase of a stable machine. There are few tests the uninitiated can perform on a bike to determine its stability, but checking with other riders will tell you a lot. Does this motorcycle handle well? Does it have a reputation for taking corners easily? For "tracking" well? (Tracking means running straight down the road without wanting to wander off at odd moments.) Besides reputation, there are a couple of things you can look for, wheelbase length being one.

Although there is some argument on this point, I have found in my riding that the longer the wheelbase of the bike, the more likely it is to be stable. Neck rake has an effect on stability also, but it is tricky. Generally, the more the neck is raked — kicked out, as in choppers — the more stable the bike will be at high speeds, and the harder it will handle at low ones. A really radical chopper will track as though it is on rails when cruising, but you have to get off and throw it around corners in the city.

The most important aspect of a bike's design, from the viewpoint of stability, is its center of gravity, of which I spoke earlier. The centers of gravity on each make and model vary widely. All other factors being equal, the bike with the lowest midpoint of engine weight will have the lowest center of gravity. This is one of the reasons that the BMWs are so smooth and stable; their massive engines are built low, with the cylinders laid out flat and near the ground.

When choosing your mount, determine its stability by learning as much technical information about it as possible, by gathering information on its performance from other riders, and by test-riding it yourself, which is covered in the next chapter.

Power

The first thing you must know about power is that there are many kinds of it, and that you cannot always accept the manufacturer's statement of a given machine's power. Especially, you must be skeptical of the dealer's glowing phrases, for he must feed the kids and his tongue is forked. There are many ways of measuring horsepower, and many more ways of utilizing it, so that 15 horsepower may mean 15 at the rear wheel, 15 in the transmission, 15 on the dynamometer, or even 15 at the brake!

In any case, it may *not* mean 15 horsepower that you can use. Power is transferred by the transmission and is set up to do specific jobs. A cowtrailing bike has a great deal of low-end torque, allowing it to pull its way out of mudholes and over stumps. But it won't go very fast. A roadracer will clip 160 mph on a straight stretch, but won't pull its own weight from a dead stop in high gear.

Every engine has a power band, which is the range of revolutions per minute in which it does efficient work. These power bands differ from one make of bike to another. The coupling of power band to gear ratios determines a bike's power characteristics.

The characteristics desirable to the nomad are: sufficient torque to move well under a load, sufficient power to give the rider a safety margin, sufficient range of power band to keep the "work" load on the engine within acceptable limits.

You must allow yourself a 30 percent margin of power when choosing your mount. That is, it must have enough power to pull 30 percent more weight than you want to put on it and to go 30 percent faster than you intend to cruise. If you intend to run at 70, carrying 250 pounds of gear (including you), you need a bike whose engine will push you down the road at 100 mph with 300 pounds aboard. If you want to waltz along the country roads at 45, with 160 pounds on top, you will need a bike that can carry 200 pounds at 60 mph.

When considering power, then, you must look both to engine size and to the way the engine's power is utilized. It is not enough to have a monster engine in your mount. If the machine is set up as a stoplight shotgun, it may not have the high-end torque to carry you and your house up those six-mile grades in the Canadian highlands.

We have determined thus far that the ideal nomad's mount will be heavier than the load it must carry, will have enough of the right kind of power to keep some in reserve, and will be stable at the speeds it is intended for. It will have a low center of gravity and a reputation for handling well.

Now let's look at a few more desirable characteristics.

Brakes

Brakes are the most neglected items on motorcycles, both by the manufacturers and the riders. It seems that the builders of motorcycles have gone out of their way to provide their products with the bare minimum in stopping power. This is somewhat understandable, in that industry responds only when pushed by the consumer and, until recently, that was a light push indeed. I have seen otherwise intelligent men get on 75-horsepower monsters capable of doing 120 mph and blast into traffic without even pulling back the brake lever to see if there is a cable attached to it! The extent of the average rider's brake maintenance is a quick glance at the wheels to see if the brake drums are still there and an occasional tightening of the cables and rods. Then, too, until very recently, front brakes (which are 60 percent more useful than the rear ones) were not even required in most states.

The simple fact is that more accidents are caused by improperly used or inadequate brakes than by any other factor.

For any rider, choosing a machine with inadequate brakes or misusing those brakes is dangerous and stupid. For the two-wheel nomad, it is unforgivable. There is a definite moral responsibility involved in piloting something that can crash into a person or object with a force of several tons. While we are each entitled to go to hell in the handbasket of our own choosing, we are not entitled to take unwilling participants with us.

There are two kinds of brakes: drum and disc. Drum

brakes operate thus: One or more curved metal "shoes" are mounted inside a "drum," which is part of the wheel. Pressure on the braking lever causes these shoes to expand outward and contact the inner face of the drum. The friction thus produced stops the bike. The shoes are faced with special compounds that are designed to wear off at a given rate and to absorb and disperse heat.

Disc brakes consist of a metal plate, or disc, that is mounted to the wheel, and a set of calipers mounted on the disc. Pressure on the brake lever closes the calipers on the disc and produces the friction to stop the bike. Inside the calipers are "pucks" that serve the same purpose as the facing on the shoes of drum brakes: they wear at a given rate and disperse heat.

Disc brakes are infinitely superior to drum brakes. They are simpler in construction, easier to service and repair, cost less to manufacture, wear longer, and are more resistant to fade and slippage than drum brakes. By 1975 I expect to see disc brakes replace drums entirely, but for now you will find them on less than 25 percent of the bikes being manufactured — and at that, mostly as front brake only.

Heat and moisture are the enemies of a bike's anchors. Heat causes "fade," or a reduction of efficiency. It occurs when you use your brakes repeatedly and rapidly or for an extended period of time. On a long, twisting downgrade, you can lose as much as 80 percent of your braking power through fade. Ganesh once lost all braking capacity six miles into a nine-mile hill outside Bennington, Vermont, and BMWs have among the best brakes in the business. They simply faded away under the strain of continually trying to hold me, Agneta, and the bike back against a 28-degree grade. (For what to do in that situation, see Chapter Fourteen.)

Moisture causes slippage. This has precisely the same

effect as fade; it leaves you without stopping power. In drum brakes, moisture is usually the result of condensation. Most drum brakes are pretty adequately protected from rain and the odd stream-fording. In disc brakes, moisture is more often caused by external water than by condensation. This is because disc brakes are open to the weather.

However, disc brakes stop you better, wet or dry. When choosing your mount, try for disc brakes, at least on the powerful front brake and preferably on both.

Note that there are a few companies manufacturing disc brake conversion kits for bikes not so equipped. They are expensive, but definitely worth considering if your chosen doesn't have supergrabbers.

Remember that a fully loaded nomadic's mount, cruising at speed, will make demands on its brakes that are far beyond the normal. When testing the brakes on your prospective bike, ask yourself if you'd feel safe with them when that cow wanders out on the road ahead of you — on a turn. If not, give thought to replacing the brakes or finding another mount.

Suspension

Suspension is important because it determines a lot of the bike's handling and stability, and most of its comfort. Suspension means the components on the bike that absorb shock. This includes the shocks themselves, the front forks, the rear swing arm, the tires, the seat, and a lot of the frame design. Some of these things, like the frame design and the swing arm, are beyond your control. Some, like the seat and tires, are adjustable or replaceable, and these are covered in Chapter Three. Some, like the shock absorbers and the front forks, can be tested for suitability.

The suspension characteristics of the forks are determined by the *amount* and *rate* of travel of the telescoping portions. Amount of travel means the distance in inches the forks travel from fully extended to fully compressed. Note, though, that your forks will seldom be fully extended. Normally they will be somewhat compressed under the weight of the bike and its load, so that what really concerns you is the *usable* amount of travel. If it is too long, your mount will be slow to recover from bumps and potholes, and this is bad. If it is too short, your suspension will bottom out, which means compress fully, and transmit the shock through the whole bike — and you.

Rate of travel means the speed at which the forks compress. Forks that compress too rapidly will not absorb shock completely and will tend to make your bike's handling mushy. Those which compress too slowly will produce a bonecruncher ride and make the handling stiff.

Manufacturers' specs will often give you the amount of travel, expressed in inches, but few can give you the rate.

Amount can best be judged by riding. It is pretty much a subjective thing and depends on your judgment of what constitutes "enough" travel. But the general rule is: the longer the distance the forks travel, the better.

Rate of travel is adjustable, within limits. This is because telescopic forks are usually of combination spring and hydraulic construction. The hydraulic part is a piston system in a tube of oil, and the rate of travel can be adjusted by changing the weight of the oil in the forks. Heavier oil gives a stiffer ride and a slower rate of travel; lighter oil gives a softer ride and a more rapid rate of travel.

The rear shocks usually work the same way, but many have an added external adjustment. Since a nomad usually loads his bike mostly to the rear, adjustable rear shocks are an important consideration. Old Ganesh was born long before externally adjustable rear shocks, and changing the oil weight is a time-consuming job, not to mention tossing $3 worth of oil into the cooking fire every time I add or subtract 50 pounds from his load.

There are two more factors you need to keep in mind: vibration and noise. These are the two great enemies of the long-range rider, and the latter is everybody's enemy.

Vibration

Vibration comes primarily from the engine. It transmits to the rider through the handlebars, the footpegs, and the saddle. A motorcycle that vibrates a lot will shake itself and you to pieces in short order. The vibration through the footpegs can actually numb your legs to the knees. This may or may not have serious consequences, depending on how lucky you are, but handlebar vibration certainly will. You haven't lived until you have to reach for the clutch in a panic situation and find your fingers too numb to close on it!

Once, in Arizona, I got off the old hooker I was riding (the bike cost me $20 every time I got on it, but had a heart of gold) and fell flat on my can. The vibration had put me to sleep from the waist down. The girl I was with laughed — until she discovered that she couldn't even get out of the saddle.

All engines vibrate. In general, two-stroke engines vibrate worse than four-strokers. However, there are exceptions in either case. The four-stroke Harley-Davidson, because of its "V" configuration and off-balance firing order, feels like the Great Los Angeles Earthquake under you, while the big Suzuki 750, a two-stroker, is one of the smoothest power plants on wheels.

The vibration that reaches you, though, is generally determined by how the engine and your contact points are mounted to the frame. The big Norton road bikes have engines that are not known for their smooth operation, but they are mounted in rubber, and this dampens their adverse effect tremendously. A number of manufacturers now mount their bike's handlebars and saddles in hard rubber, which helps a lot.

Still, there are boneshakers and there are smoothies. When choosing your mount, check with other riders on this. And don't buy anything you haven't personally tested for vibration.

Noise

Noise is disastrous. It is an insidious thing that works on the subconscious rhythms of the body and produces all sorts of ugly side effects. There have been hundreds of sociological and psychological studies done on the effects of noise on people, and they have universally agreed that these effects are all negative. It is a toss-up whether noise or vibration contributes more to rider fatigue.

Noise is a subjective thing. How much is too much? Only you can tell this, and you do it by asking yourself if you can live with a given amount of noise all day, day after day.

Finally, remember that noise is the one factor that reaches beyond you to the people and country you pass. Leaving a trail of decibels behind you is not only rude, it muddies the water for the next few hundred bikers who come along.

Noise and vibration produce two external problems related to safety. A vibrating machine causes blurred images in your mirrors, which is not good at all, and a noisy machine may not let you hear that Greyhound bus whooshing up beside you.

The last and maybe most important consideration in choosing your mount is reliability. Will it run from here to there with reasonable chances of avoiding a breakdown? Can you depend on it to cross those vast stretches of boondocks between dealers of your brand of bike?

Reliability

This has two parts: dependability of the bike and availability of repairs. If your machine breaks a lot, you will spend much time sitting around having it repaired. If it seldom breaks but there are few people who will work on it, you will sit around *waiting* to have it repaired.

You have absolutely nothing to go on in assessing a particular bike's reliability except reputation, and even then you must take what you learn with some salt. BMWs are considered to be nearly immortal, but I have seen a number of them that were lemons from day one. English bikes are thought to be "fussy," with some little thing always needing repair, but I know of a number of round-the-world Triumphs and BSAs that gave their riders zero hassle.

But the gathered opinion of many riders has weight. If you hear that a certain bike is considered reliable by most folks, you can believe that it is at least better than average.

Availability of parts and mechanics should be weighed carefully before you choose your mount. Suppose you decide that *the* bike for you is the 500 cc Mackerel Marauder, and you buy it and truck off to Mooseglue, Canada, where you bust a main shaft key. It's not a hard repair; you can do it yourself. You can also grow a beard while waiting for that new part, which has to come from the only Mackerel dealer in the Western Hemisphere, and he's located in Boca Raton, Florida.

Here's a trick: go to your local telephone company office and dig through their directories for the cities you think you will be heading for in that first year on the road. Look up "Motorcycle Dealers" in the Yellow Pages and see who carries or services the make bike you are interested in. You may be surprised at what you find. A young lady and I once found ourselves stranded in the New Mexican deserts with Ganesh complaining bitterly about a pain in his electricals. I was all set to phone Phantom Motorcycles in Los Angeles, when along came a panel truck with the lovely BMW emblem on its sides. Turned out that one of the largest and best-equipped BMW dealerships in America was not twenty miles away in Las Cruces! When we brought my odd-model antique in, they didn't bat an eyelash, and Elaina and I were back on the road to Juárez in less than two hours.

The general rule on reliability is: buy a popular machine with a wide distributorship and a reputation for reliability. Pat Malloy, an instructor at Los Angeles Trade Tech's motorcycle school, says that there are only four makes you can get serviced "anywhere in the world": Honda, BMW, Triumph, and Harley-Davidson. I don't know if that is still accurate, since dealer networks are expanding rapidly, but those four makes — at least — are well distributed in this country.

If selecting your mount seems a complicated process, remember that you have all the time in the world. Check and recheck your three vectors; make sure of what you need in a bike. Reread all of this chapter and content yourself that you understand the interaction of all the factors. Talk to everyone you can reach who rides distance. Read specs and technical information, invest in magazines. The few dollars you spend on research will more than pay for themselves if you avoid a single major mistake in choosing your mount.

Once you have an accurate idea of the machine you

are looking for, you are ready to go find it, and that's the subject of the next chapter.

Wisdom

"A good wife is a comfort, a good dagger a blessing, and a good mount a necessity."

— Arab saying

During the period of Goyathlay's raids on the Mexicans, he always made sure that he got the pick of the horses.

2.
THE WILY Trader

Now that you have an idea of the size and type bike you want, your next step is buying it. The first move in this process is to determine how much to spend on it.

What You Can Really Afford

Your mount will probably be the most expensive item in your system. What you must bear in mind is that it isn't the *only* item. You have yourself to outfit and the rest of your traveling home to get together. Even if you build most of your own equipment and travel light, these things will cost you money. Note also that the purchase price of your bike is not the only expense the machine will present you with.

Let us start with the total amount of money available to you and whittle away at it until we have a leftover figure with which to buy your mount.

Outfitting yourself will run from $20 to $300, depending on how completely you want to dress and how much quality you want in your purchases. You may prefer nylon to leather, cheap boots to riding boots, one pair of pants to four pairs. You may already own serviceable gear. These things will affect your outfitting costs. I have found, though, that the median figure for most two-wheel nomads is $185. Whatever the amount is for you, the important thing is to know what it is before you sink your money in other things.

Your home, depending again on amounts and quality of gear, can run you anywhere from $100 to $1,000. Do you intend to tent? If so, how much tent are you going to buy? Cook on charcoal or a three-burner Coleman? Flashlight or candles or a propane unit? The variables are enormous, and you must be fairly accurate in your estimates. Think these things through for a few days. Make lists. Compare prices. A dollar saved — without sacrifice of quality or need — is a dollar toward your motorcycle.

Roughly, you can figure half your available cash for yourself and your home. The other half is for the bike, but not all of it for purchase.

Insurance is a subject steeped in myth for most of us. It is a form of betting against yourself. If you win, you lose. If you lose, sometimes you lose both ways.

But no sane person would travel without it. And it costs money. Insurance rates vary widely because there are no real parameters for motorcycles yet. You can pay anywhere from $50 to $350 a year. Check with a couple of dealers for their recommendations on specific insurance companies. Write each company for rates on the machine you have chosen. Talk to other riders about each company's pay record. My own recommendation is Elite, which is a Canadian company. They have reasonable rates and a record of prompt payment on claims. The Sources Appendix will tell you how to find their address.

Licensing fees are not much, but they are unavoidable. You won't get very far down the road without a tag on the back. Fees run from $3 in some states to about $12 in others.

Cash is the most versatile tool in the world. It will take any shape you need. There are times when no other tool will solve the problem as precisely as folding money, and you must carry some of this with you. The amount is up to you, but the more you have, the more leverage your tool will offer.

Finally, if you plan to buy a used machine, no matter how clean, you will need a reserve of cash for those things you will find out only after you have bought the bike. As a general rule, you need 20 percent of the purchase price for repairs and modifications to your bike.

What you have, then, with which to buy your bike is what you have left over after you have bought your own gear, your home, your insurance and licensing, and laid aside some for repairs and modifications. This brings up the next major decision: new bike or used?

New or Used?

Any new motorcycle will run you in excess of $400, and a big tourer can cost upwards of $2,400. This initial cost is the single biggest drawback to the "new bike" option. There are some others. Few bikes come factory-equipped with the particular accessories you want and changing them will cost you money. It is one thing to toss out the saddle, handlebars, and shock absorbers on a bike you have paid a secondhand price for, but quite another to do so with a shiny-new bike. Also, a new bike must be broken in, which is a slow process. If you are hot to get down the road, this can be an aggravating thing and might lead to your fudging on the break-in requirements — which will lead to serious problems later in your mount's life, usually at an uncomfortable moment. Finally, having a new mount under you affects your head in some strange ways, and this can have repercussions. I know of an experienced nomad who nearly killed himself because he refused to lay his machine down in a critical situation that called for that reaction. His bike was a month old and he didn't want to scratch the paint! As a result, he bent the frame, destroyed his forks, and broke two ribs.

Why buy new, then?

Several reasons, the first of which is that you know what you are getting for your money. With a new mount you risk only the inefficiencies of the manufacturer and the oversights of the dealer, rather than a history of misuse that has echoed throughout the internals of the machine. With a new bike, the problems are usually of the adjustment and loose-connection variety. You will seldom find a major malfunction in a new machine. If you do, you usually have recourse in the form of your warranty. Of course, "warranty" is a term that allows more hedging than "guarantee," and that's why you get the one instead of the other. But even a warranty offers more protection than you get buying secondhand. There is an old saw that a warranty is only as good as the dealer who gives it, and that is a thing to bear in mind also. Fortunately, most dealers today are pretty good about honoring their warranties, though some must be persuaded.

There are two other advantages to buying your mount new, one small, one large. The small advantage is that new bikes come with tool kits and handbooks, and while the tools in an average bike's kit aren't the best quality, they are the right tools for that bike, and a balanced selection. If you have ever bought tools, you know how quickly the cost can grow. And it isn't always possible to get a handbook for a secondhand bike, especially the older models. The large advantage I mentioned is that when you buy new there is a much wider range of makes and models available. If you have decided, for example, that a BSA Gold Star is the right mount for you, you may not be able to find one used. Or worse, you may find a dog and be tempted to buy it anyway.

So: a new bike costs a lot and will probably put your head on sideways for a while, *but* it will be reliable, will give you some protection in case of factory foul-ups, and will offer you a much broader base from which to choose.

What about a used bike?

The basic rule on buying used motorcycles is: don't. Experienced buyers get taken every day. Entire books have been written on the subject. At best, it's a gamble. At worst, it can be a disaster. The *only* value there is in buying your mount "previously appreciated" is saving money. And if you pick a loser you aren't going to save a cent.

Still, enough people luck out to make used bikes attractive. I bought Ganesh not only used, but about sixth-hand. He had about a quarter of a million miles on him, had been on three of the five continents, and was overloaded with jury-rigged wiring and gadgets. I paid $500 for him, and in the years that we have been friends have spent less than $200 for parts and repairs. Nothing internal or major has broken.

While there are no hard and fast rules for separating the cream puffs from the lemons, you stand a better chance of winning if you go armed with some basic knowledge. Here's what to look for in used bikes . . .

First, put yourself in the right frame of mind. A motorcycle is not a thing to buy on impulse, and this applies doubly to used machines. Know *exactly* what you are looking for and do not accept substitutes, no matter how tempting. Approach the seller of your potential mount as though he were a pit of vipers. Discount all that you are told unless you can personally verify it. Better to wrong this person unfairly than to go to prison for murdering him later. Remember to translate from the English: "The bike was just overhauled" means "I set the tappets and poured some motor-honey in it yesterday."

Know as much as possible about the quirks of the particular machine you have settled on. Does it leak oil? Idle roughly? Wobble in the turns? In some bikes, these are natural design flaws and no reason to discount your potential friend. Read everything printed on the make and model bike you are after. Talk to owners and riders of the machine. The Suzuki 750 is considered top-heavy by most riders and wobbles at low speeds, but it is a fine tourer. Harley-Davidsons have a rough vibration from the engine, but it is due to the design, not a malfunction. Triumphs are prone to valve clatter, which to the untutored ear sounds like half the engine preparing to come through the cylinder heads but which actually indicates a healthy engine. If you do not know the peculiarities of your chosen bike, you will come to grief when it gets down to buying or leaving.

When you have yourself mentally in hand, go find your bike. Then consider each of the following points:

General inspection. Walk around the bike and study it *closely* for signs of misuse. Look for dents and scratches. Check the paint. Is it new? If so, why? Could be simply to make the bike more salable, but it could also be to cover up the marks of a crash. If it has new paint, has the whole bike been done or just certain sections? Chances are that a complete repaint is cosmetic but a partial conceals some abuse to the bike. Check the levers. Are the ends ground off or scarred? This indicates that the bike has been dropped. Likewise, check the side cases on the engine. Scratches mean a dropped bike. Gouges and ground-off spots mean a dragged bike. Ask the owner how the machine came by its scars. Listen more to how honest his answer feels than to what he says. If you don't think you'd trust him with your future, smile and move on. This is important because there are many things that even a mechanic cannot spot without tools, and these can be dangerous later. A bent frame, for example, can be straightened enough to pass visual inspection, repainted, and seem good as new. But if it is even slightly off it will eventually destroy your transmission, your wheel bearings, your steering races, and maybe you.

After a thorough visual inspection, get in there and get your hands dirty. Look at the odometer and judge whether the indicated mileage agrees with the general condition of the bike. If it doesn't, find out why. Look at the metal parts for rust and pitting. A poorly maintained bike is not likely to have good innards, either.

Move to the front of the machine and look at the wheel. Is the tire worn unevenly? If so, it can indicate anything from a bent frame to improperly aligned axles. Test the spokes for tension. Loose spokes show poor maintenance. Run your finger, or preferably a piece of metal, around the spokes. They should all sound nearly the same pitch, which shows proper tension.

Put the bike on its center stand or on a block, so that the front wheel is clear of the ground. Now, face the bike, straddle the wheel, and clamp your knees. Grab the handlebars and turn them from side to side. Does the wheel move surely or does it have play? If there is play, you have a dangerous front end. It may be a matter of adjustments and tightenings, but it could be worn bearings, worn shocks, a cracked triple tree, or any number of other things that will keep you awake nights. And while you are in this silly position on the front of the bike, look at the cables and housings on the handlebars. I have found that wear most often occurs on the front side of the cables. Look for cracked rubber in the housings, rusted or torn cables, and bent metal in the parts that attach the cables to the levers. None of these conditions are fatal, but they are an expense if they have to be fixed and are another indication of the care the previous owner has given the bike.

Move to the rear wheel, with the bike still on the stand. Squat down and eyeball the bike. Are the wheels in line? Does it look as if the line through the frame is true? If not, check the rear axle to see if it is adjusted properly. Chain-driven motorcycles all adjust by moving the rear axle forward or back, and quite often this is done incorrectly, with one side of the axle being moved farther than the other. While you are there, look for grease leaks where the axle enters the wheel. This can indicate worn seals or bearings.

With the bike still on its stand, spin the rear wheel. Does it run true? If not, why not? Check it for spoke tension as you did the front wheel. Check the rim for dents. A dented rim means the bike hit something pretty hard, which could mean interior damage in the suspension system. Also, a bent rim means a poorly seated tire, and that's not good.

Sit directly behind the bike and look at the shocks. Are they vertical? That is, is there a vertical line from their upper mount on the frame to their lower mount on the axle? Out-of-line shocks indicate side collisions or a bad fall.

Now check the chain. Chain condition can tell you a great deal about how the bike has been used and maintained. Look for rust on the links and for worn or pitted metal. Both indicate bad maintenance. There should be, on a well-kept chain, a light film of clean oil, with no dirt or grit in it. A chain is a complex systems of rollers, bearings, and linkages that goes through a lot of reciprocal motion. Dirt is almost as disastrous to a chain as to an engine. While you are here, check the rear sprocket for broken or worn teeth, general cleanliness, and uneven wear on one side or the other of the plate, which indicates improper alignment and/or a bent frame.

Now move around to the side of the bike, preferably

the one with the chain on it. Do another visual inspection, concentrating on the change of perspective you achieved by walking around the bike. Look at the undersides of things. Wear? Dirt? Rust? Missing or fresh paint? If the owner has offered you a clean and polished machine with caked oil under the engine, you can bet that the rest of his maintenance has been of the same surface-only variety.

Check the chain again, this time for play. A properly adjusted chain should have about an inch of up-and-down play on its *upper* run, midway between the sprockets. You measure the upper run because that is the power-transfer run. The lower run takes no tension. An improperly adjusted chain shows a lack of even basic maintenance. A good way to tell if the bike's owner has made a practice of keeping a slack chain is to examine the parts of the frame and accessories that pass near the chain. Are there wear marks or worn spots on them?

Now, move to the engine and transmission. Look deep in the cooling fins for dirt and oil. Check the places where the cylinder heads join the body and the engine mates to the transmission. Oil? Discoloration? These show worn gaskets, cracked metal, and general abuse. Pull the plugs — all of them. They should be a consistent color, a light grayish brown. Caked deposits on the plugs, burned spots, and a wide variation in condition from plug to plug indicate an improperly cared-for engine, which will eventually cost you trouble. Look at the exhaust system. Is there oil leakage or discoloration around the place where the pipes exit the engine? (Note: the pipes themselves will be discolored. This is natural in any bike with more than a thousand miles on it and doesn't indicate anything bothersome.)

Pull the dipstick and look at the oil. It should be clean and clear. Dirty oil, old oil, show bad maintenance on its most costly level. Oil is the blood of an engine, and bad blood will show, sooner or later. Feel for grit or metal shavings in the oil. Neither is good. Smell the oil. Does it smell burned? Burned oil indicates bad rings and a potential major engine rebuild.

If all is within allowable limits so far, you are ready to start the bike. Feel the engine to see if it has been prewarmed, which would indicate that the owner is not anxious to have you try it cold. Then back off and let him start the bike for you. Does it start with a reasonable amount of effort? Every bike has its own starting personality, and its own rituals for cranking up. But all should be startable without raising sweat on your lip. How does the bike sound? Do you hear expensive noises inside? Does it sound nervous? Is it idling at a reasonable speed or running fast just to keep running? A good bike will start easily, idle smoothly, and make consistent sounds from inside.

Walk to the rear and look at the exhaust. Is there smoke? Two-stroke engines produce smoke naturally, but it should be light in both amount and color. Four-strokers should not produce smoke after a very short warm-up period. If your potential mount has two pipes, check for equal amounts and color of smoke. Place your hands a few inches behind the outlets — far enough back to avoid being burned — and feel the compression. It should be equal or nearly so from both pipes. Likewise, each should be about the same temperature. Hot exhaust means hot cylinder. Look into the pipes. Are they the same color inside? Do they look oily? Is oil or gasoline dripping from one of them?

Now, go sit on the bike. Familiarize yourself with the gearshift and clutch, the brakes and throttle. With the rear wheel clear of the ground, put the bike into each gear and see how smoothly it transfers from one to the other. Everything good so far? Okay, take it for a ride.

Look first for smoothness and consistency in the operation of the machine. Does it shift gears uncomplainingly, without missing shifts or grinding and clunking? A number of bikes clunk naturally when going into or out of low gear, most notably the big road bikes. Ganesh sounds like a Sherman tank in the rutting season, but in him it's normal. Look particularly to the engine's responsiveness. Does it hesitate or complain when you crank the throttle or change gears? These are bad signs because they indicate general loss of power and approaching senility. Do the controls operate well, without hanging fire or being mushy? How much effort does it take to hold the clutch lever in, or the brake lever? What kind of pressure do you have to exert to make the machine change directions or speeds? If they are excessive, best move on to another mount.

Test your brakes by making a series of stops in succession, starting out at low speed and building up. If your anchors don't grab surely and smoothly every time, you'll have to add the cost of shoes or drums or both to the asking price of the bike.

If your mount runs, goes, and stops satisfactorily at this point, check the handling and suspension. Take the cycle to a nice rough place and run over it a few times. The shocks should not bottom out unless you really clip a pothole. How does the ride feel on a rough road? Could you live with it for an extended period?

Take your machine around some curves. Do this at low speed and traveling fast. Is there a difference in handling characteristics at different speeds? If so, what sort? A good mount will follow a smooth line through a curve. It will not wobble or pull to one side. A bike that does this, whether it is misuse or design flaw that causes it, is a poor bet for you. Leaning through a turn is an operation the motorcycle nomad will do thousands of times, and it can be either a graceful, unconscious move or a piece of work. If your mount does not feel sure and happy in a turn, it will be a disaster to live on.

If, at this point, you are convinced that you have found your mount, take it back to the owner and leave it. Go home and let the little things that bugged you grow and give you insomnia. If the bike still looks good in the morning, go get it.

Sources of information: Everything printed on the bike you want. Other riders. Road tests on your make and vintage bike.

Wisdom

"When buying a camel, look more to the seller than the beast."

— Bedouin saying

"The Cherokee are great traders but the white men are great liars. This is why the white men own Tennessee."

— Charlie Blackhand

"This car carries our famous 100 percent warranty. When it breaks . . . that is, if it breaks, just bring it in and we'll fix it free, except for parts."

— TV commercial

3.

SADDLING UP

The next step in getting ready to tour is rigging your mount for the road. "Rigging" means fitting the bike with the proper combination of parts and accessories to carry you and your gear down the highway in maximum comfort and safety.

Note that comfort and safety mean different things to different people. I have met individuals who were quite happy to joust with the twenty-ton trucks while mounted on trail bikes. Some of them even seemed sane.

But I will stress the word *maximum* and speak in terms of the ideal rig.

The factors involved in rigging a bike for the road are: rider comfort, carrying capacity, and high-speed stability. All parts and accessories you put on your mount must maximize one or more of these factors. You must choose the right handlebars, footpegs, and saddle to keep you comfortable over long periods. You must design your storage system to distribute weight evenly and to reduce windloading (see Chapter Eleven). You must select the right fairing to stabilize your bike at freeway speeds. Your tires must not only be capable of handling the whole range of surface conditions you expect to encounter but of doing so under a heavy load.

It is obvious that some choices are more important than others. You need to spend more thought on a fairing than on handlebars; more thought on your tires than on which set of footpegs you need; more thought on storage systems than on which size mirrors to buy. The order of priority is: safety, comfort, carrying capacity.

I will therefore take the parts and accessories in descending order of importance.

Tires

Tires are the one place where you cannot compromise. Your life literally depends on the four square inches of rubber that touch the road. A bad choice of tread, a compromise on quality, poor maintenance — these can be fatal. Become friendly with your tries. The Danakil nomads of Ethiopia say, "He who tends his own feet before those of his horse will soon have no feet to tend." This is a good attitude to adopt toward your own mount's "feet." Buy them with care, treat them with respect, and give them the constant attention the aerialist gives his trapeze.

When selecting new tires, look first to tread design, then to brand name. Tread design will determine the suitability of the tire for touring, and brand name guarantees quality. Tread design means the pattern of grooves and notches on the part of the tire that touches the road. There are numerous designs, each carefully engineered for a specific purpose. Knobbies are for off-road riding. Slicks are for drag-racing. Universals are compromise designs halfway between dirt and road tires.

What you want are plain road or touring tires. These tires have tread designs meant to cope with sustained high-speed running. They will not function as well as knobbies in the dirt, nor as well as street tires when plodding through the downtown traffic. But dirt and traffic form a small part of the nomad's riding. His concern is with the open road, and for this, road tires are supreme.

When buying, specify the approximate weight load your mount will carry. The dealer will know what you need.

Look for tires with sufficient side tread to allow you to lean the bike way over in turns or emergencies. Test this by standing the tire on the floor and tilting it over 45 degrees. If you have tread touching the floor, you can use the tire. Buy four- or six-ply tires. Two-ply tires are an invitation to a blowout.

Most of the worth of a tire is on the inside. You cannot tell how well a tire is built by looking at it. Therefore, buy a known brand. There are many, among which are Goodyear, Avon, Dunlop, Bridgestone, Continental and Royal. I wear Dunlop Gold Seal K 70s on Ganesh, front and rear.

Some British and American tire manufacturers now have their tires built in Japan. Others, like Dunlop, build some themselves and have some built in Japan. It is possible to get a lot of tires in either "Japanese" or "English" versions, although the manufacturers do not specify this in their ads. I have found that the Japanese-built tires wear out a little more rapidly but have better road-holding capacity. More "stick." Given the choice, I will buy Japanese versions of my tires.

The rule on buying used tires is: don't. A used or recapped tire is never a bargain because you do not know where it has been. But if you have bought your mount in a "previously appreciated" condition, chances are that it has used rubber on it. This is how you check that rubber out:

Tread. If your tires have less than a quarter of an inch depth from the bottom of the grooves to the top of the remaining tread, change them. If there are gaps in the pattern, or worn spots, or one side of the pattern with more wear than the other, change them.

Wear. The sides of the tire may have a network of

minute cracks. This is not dangerous unless the cracks are deep enough to stick something in. The two things to look for are wear or cracks where the tire meets the rim of the wheel and crumbly or powdery rubber. Cracks around the rim are caused by dry rot and accumulated dirt and grit. Crumbly or powdery rubber indicates ultraviolet damage and old age. The best way to approach a used tire is to ask yourself if you would feel safe on it during a panic stop in a rainstorm. If you do not think you could be that friendly with the tire, change it.

Tires cost between $20 and $30.

More information can be found in the Sources Appendix.

Fairings

Fairings are fiber-glass windbreakers that fit over the front of your bike and have windshields on top. They come in two varieties, handlebar-mounted and frame-mounted. Bar-mounted fairings are usually "partials," which extend to just below the headlight and protect you down to the knees. Frame-mounted fairings are usually "full," extending to the bottom of the bike's frame and offering complete rider protection.

Fairings have several functions besides the obvious one of keeping the rain and bugs off you. Because they improve the aerodynamics of your mount, fairings will give you a 5 to 10 percent increase in gas mileage and a corresponding increase in top speed. Ganesh got around 80 mph before I put a fairing on him, and now gets 91 mph. Mileage went from 42 per gallon to nearly 50.

A frame-mounted fairing will protect you and your mount should you go down. I once saw a nomad in Oklahoma drop his Butler-Avon rigged BSA at 70 mph and come up with nothing worse than a ground-off corner on the fairing.

But the two prime functions of fairings are as follows: First, a fairing breaks the wind and puts you in a zone of quiet air. This allows you to sit back and enjoy the scenery instead of grimly hanging on through a 60 to 80 mph head wind. It also allows you to ride in an upright position instead of a roadracer's crouch. Over an extended run, these are vital concerns. Second, a frame-mounted fairing will tend to stabilize your mount at speed, taking much of the work out of riding. These two factors combine to reduce the fatigue element by a significant amount. You will find that you can do a given distance with much less effort or a greater distance for the same wear and tear on yourself when your bike has a fairing.

There are some drawbacks to fairings. They are expensive, cannot be found secondhand, and are not usually transferable if you swap bikes. They are also noisy, being reflecting surfaces. A fairing will magnify every whisper of each valve into a rattle and bounce it into your face. This is not much of a problem with partial fairings, but can really make itself felt with full fairings. With a partial, expect a 15 percent increase in engine noise. With a full, expect from 25 to 35 percent, depending on the make and model.

Some people also believe a fairing makes your bike look funny. But then, some people think Raquel Welch looks funny. I have gotten used to kids pointing and making comments about Batmobiles and such.

The advantages of having a fairing so far outweigh the disadvantages that most people who have ridden behind one would never again ride without.

How do you tell a good fairing from a bad one? Again, buy a reputable make. Fairings are made of fiber glass, which is a new technology. Mistakes are still being made, usually at the expense of the buyer. Fiber glass takes its strength from the distribution of stress along the lengths of cloth used in manufacturing the fairing. Long strips, strong fairing; short strips, weak fairing. Reputable manufacturers use cloth in lengths up to two feet and hand-lay these in the mold. Less reputable manufacturers spray the mold with a mixture of chopped fiber glass and resins, then hand-lay longer cloth over this. Short of sawing the fairing in half, you cannot tell one method from the other. Until it is too late.

Another reason for buying a known brand involves warpage. All fiber glass warps slightly when taken out of the mold. The better manufacturers compensate for this. A lot of less reputable manufacturers pirate their designs from the better makers, building molds off finished fairings bought from their more conscientious brethren. This results in a fairing which has two to three times the warpage that a good one has and which is going to be next to useless on your bike. Often dangerously useless.

Partial fairing or full? Partials are less expensive, easier to mount, and do not look as cumbersome as full fairings. But most partials are bar-mounted, and that presents a problem. A bar-mounted fairing turns with the handlebars. At high speed, it will tend to shimmy, which will translate directly to the wheel. If you have strong arms and good control, this is only an annoyance. But if the shimmy gets out of hand it can turn into frame oscillation, producing a high-speed wobble.

Full fairings are all frame-mounted, as far as I know. They are more costly than partials, but are worth it. Any fairing will improve the handling of your bike, but the difference is more pronounced with a full.

There are a number of good makes available. I would choose from the following: Butler-Avon, Wixom, Vetter, Califia, Bates, and Fibre-Mold. Butler-Avon made the first frame-mounted touring fairings, and they still make top-quality products, distinctively styled and flawlessly crafted. Wixom, the most copied line of fairings in the world, makes the best bar-mounted fairings. If Wixom says a given fairing will fit your bike, it will. You won't have a headlight that splays all over the sidewalk. They also offer thirty or forty metal-flake colors. Bates makes simple, businesslike fairings that fit most everything and are constructed with a degree of care approaching fanaticism. Califia makes a series of exotic-looking fairings that have an amazing number of extras you can add, including stereo tape decks and cigarette lighters. Fibre-Mold makes a sturdy fairing called the Tourmaster. It has rubber mounts and is the most vibration-free fairing I've seen.

I believe that Craig Vetter makes the best fairings in the world. Vetter fairings are superbly built and engineered, well finished, and offer some unique advantages. All Vetters come with built-in pockets, which gives you a place to put all those things you normally have to scrabble for while riding. The Windjammer series comes with vents in the windshield for rider comfort, a built-in 50-watt headlight, and optional tonneau covers for the pockets. All Vetters are of one-piece construction, which makes them extremely strong and aerodynamically sound. I have had an old Vetter Phantom on Ganesh for almost two years and would not trade it for anything on the market.

In choosing your fairing, look for width. The thing should be wide enough to cover your hands and prevent air from flowing up your sleeves. A number of the British fairings, particularly the Butler-Avons, are very narrow, which pleases the European rider but which most American riders will find uncomfortable.

Fairings cost from $45 up for partials, and from $100 up for fulls. Expect to pay double that for the better models.

Information available from the manufacturers, whose addresses are in the Sources Appendix.

Handlebars, Saddles, Footpegs

These are a set. They interact to produce a comfortable or comfortless ride. I will start with the saddle.

There are as many styles of saddle as there are manufacturers of bikes. All differ slightly, but all that come on touring or road machines are suitable for you. Saddles are interchangeable from bike to bike in that they can be altered by welding to fit the mounts on your machine. If the saddle on your bike does not suit you, find one that does and have it fitted.

A touring bike needs as low a saddle as possible. This is to keep the center of gravity down. But do not sacrifice saddle thickness to gain an extra inch.

The correct height for a touring saddle is determined by the relative positions of your legs and feet. With your feet on the pegs, your thighs should be nearly horizontal; at the same time, you should be able to rest your feet flat on the ground while seated.

The shape of your saddle is also important. It needs to be wide enough at the rump to support your weight on your hips, not the inside of your thighs. It must be narrow enough in front to allow you free use of your legs without chafing.

Firmness is a matter of personal taste, but in general, the firmer the better. A thin saddle will help you find all your bones in a short time.

Finally, a good touring saddle will allow you to scoot back and forth at least six inches without sacrificing "reach" to the controls and pegs.

There are only two things to know about handlebars: do not buy "chopper" bars and set your bars at the correct height. Chopper bars are those with radical bends or welds. Bars with radical bends will bend under stress. Welded bars will break under stress. Neither of these characteristics is desirable, especially while running down the road.

To find the correct height for your bars, sit on your bike with your feet on the ground. Pick a point on the ground about eight feet ahead of your front wheel and reach for it with both arms. The point in the air where your hands are is where your bars belong. This position will keep your arms low enough to avoid fatigue and the temptation to "hang" on the bars and high enough to keep your back straight while riding. If, for reasons of finance or insanity, you do not have a fairing, your bars should be two to three inches lower than this, and, if possible, two inches narrower between the handgrips.

Footpegs are fairly standard, and on many machines cannot be altered. If you can alter yours, find the thickest, toughest make around and mount them. Most footpegs attach directly to the frame and so transmit engine vibration to your legs. Vibration is one of the most fatiguing elements of two-wheel nomading, and anything you can do to reduce it will make you a happier rider.

If your pegs are adjustable, set them so that you have two or three inches of foot movement while maintaining control of the shift and brake levers.

When you have set up your saddle, footpegs, and handlebars correctly, you will have an upright riding position, with your thighs parallel to the ground and your arms in a relaxed curve. You will be able to shift your weight readily to either side and to the rear of the bike. And you will be able to place both feet on the ground without strain.

Saddles: Best are BMW USA Touring, Bates Solo, and Harley-Davidson Tractor. All are findable secondhand or purchasable new. From $8 to $65.

Handlebars: Anything off a street or road bike of

known brand. Anything from an accessory house that is specifically designated as a "touring" design. Expect to pay from $4 to $16 new.

Footpegs: Any make, thickest rubber available. $4 to $8 new.

Information: Talk with other riders.

Mirrors

Mirrors are not mandatory in all states or countries, but they should be. Like helmets, they are precautionary insurance. No experienced nomad will ride without at least one, and most use two.

There are two types of bike mirror. The first type mounts on a metal rod and adjusts at the mirror itself. The second mounts through the end of the handlebar and usually adjusts at the mount as well as at the mirror. The second variety is the best. Rod-mounted mirrors vibrate more than those that mount through the bar ends. Vibration is the enemy of vision in a mirror. If you choose a rod-mounted mirror, get the shortest rod available and mount your mirror as low on it as feasible. End-mounted mirrors are not usually adjustable for length, but they do not need to be.

Make sure that your mirror has a large enough surface to give you vision in two lanes and that it is mounted in such a position to give you some viewing range directly behind you. If you have two mirrors, set them up to overlap fields of vision slightly.

Convex mirrors give you a larger field of view but distort the apparent distance of that truck behind you. This is because of the parallax effect produced by your eyes striking a curved surface. Oncoming vehicles seem much farther back when viewed in a convex mirror. For this reason, I avoid convex mirrors.

I have two bar-mounted mirrors on Ganesh. They are

adjustable eight ways, are almost vibrationless, and cost $8 each. They are standard mirrors off a Mercedes Benz 220, and I have never found anything to equal them. I had a welder adapt them to my bars for $2.

Since you cannot shift around as far on a bike as in a car, night glare is a real problem. There are no bike mirrors with day/night adjustments, and riding several hours with a following vehicle's headlights in your eyes can be discouraging. The cure for this is a pair of women's nylon footlets. Stretched over your mirrors, they cut the glare completely and leave a distortion-free image of the lights behind.

Mirrors: Any make that fits your bike. $2.98 to $8.

Information: Magazine ads. Sources Appendix.

Storage Systems

The final consideration in rigging your bike for the road is the storage system. The elements of a bike storage system are: luggage rack, tank pack, seat storage, and side storage. The factors involved are weight distribution and windloading.

Weight distribution deserves close attention. There are two radically different kinds of weight you will put on your mount. The first is you and your passenger. This is "live" weight. It can react to the shifts in acceleration and deceleration that your mount makes, thus compensating for changes in the center of gravity. The second kind is "dead" weight — that which is strapped to your mount and is inert. All of your gear except the clothes on your back falls into this category. And deadweight, no matter how it is arranged or tied down, affects the handling, performance, and stopping power of your bike.

The effects of deadweight can be minimized by careful distribution of that weight. Ideally, all deadweight should

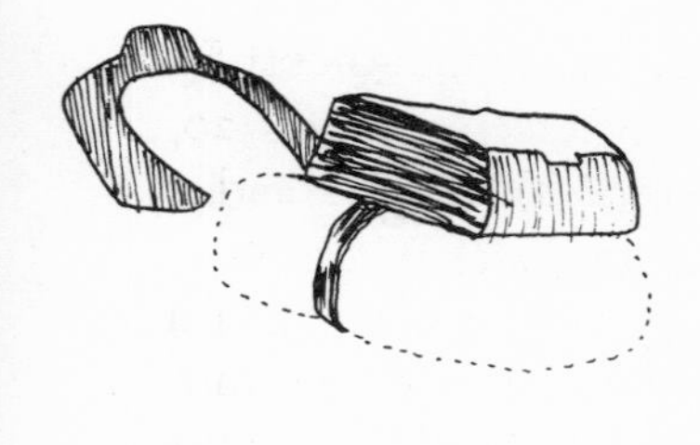
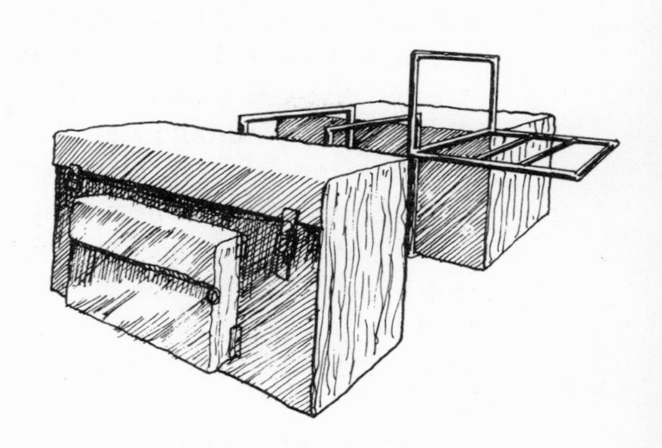

Left to right: fairing pocket, tank pack, soft saddle bags, and luggage rack.

be located directly between the wheels and near the ground. Unfortunately, this area is usually occupied by the engine and transmission. The next best thing would be to divide the weight equally between the front and rear portions of the bike. But this would have a bad effect on the steering geometrics, not to mention the problem of night riding with a bedroll over your headlight.

The solution is a compromise, wherein you attempt to hang your gear as low as possible on either side of the rear wheel and to put the lighter material on the saddle behind you. There are certain problems inherent in this system, none of which have been fully solved. Saddles are not stable surfaces and are difficult to strap anything to securely. If you use a solo saddle and put a rack behind you, where will you put that friend you are hoping to meet somewhere down the highway?

The average road bike is set up so that the weight distribution with one rider aboard is roughly 50–50. That is, half the weight on each wheel. It is your goal to come as close to that 50–50 as possible when you have rigged and packed your bike.

The elements of a storage rig begin with luggage racks.

Luggage racks are chromed metal decks that attach to the frame of your bike and run from the back of the seat out over the rear fender. Most street and touring bikes come equipped with them. Racks are conveniences. They are meant to carry a jacket or a briefcase. At most, a small suitcase. The problem with racks is that many riders overload them. A luggage rack is absolutely the worst position for deadweight. It places the load high up and far back of the center of gravity, causing it to lever up the front end of the machine.

However, when used properly, a luggage rack is a thing of much purpose. Proper usage is covered in Chapter Eleven.

Tank packs are bags that strap to the top of your mount's gas tank. Their prime function is to provide handy storage of maps, gloves, cigarettes, etc. They also serve to transfer deadweight forward, aiding in weight distribution. There are sizes and makes to fit almost any need. In general, the bigger the better. The really big tank packs will hold an amazing amount of gear and keep it all handy. The best makes are Corona, MBI, and Letherwerks. Corona's bags are heavy black vinyl, have lockable zippers, and come with a transparent map pocket on top. MBI's bags are made of Naugahyde, can be converted to backpacks, and are really huge. Letherwerks's bags are individually crafted by Joel Wood, are custom-fitted to your bike, and are immaculately finished in latigo hide.

Seat storage is not properly a part of your bike's rigging since it utilizes the saddle and is not a separate piece of equipment. But every nomad I know uses this area when not carrying a passenger. There is nothing wrong with strapping gear behind you except that it will have a tendency to shift around and will thus be a constant drain on your attention. I have also found that continuous or repeated use of bunji cords to strap gear on the saddle results in warpage of the saddle frame.

The advantages of seat storage are, first, whatever weight you place on the saddle behind you has been compensated for in the design of your bike, and second, when properly arranged, the load can act as a back brace.

For what part of your gear to store on the saddle, and how to arrange it, see Chapter Eleven.

The major component of your weight-carrying system is your saddlebags. Saddlebags keep the deadweight as low as possible and as near the center of the suspension system as can be arranged, given the limits of motorcycle construction. Since this is where the wise nomad will carry the bulk of his deadweight, side storage units merit some thought.

Saddlebags come in either flexible or rigid form. The rigid bags are usually made of fiber glass or metal and the flexible bags are usually of canvas or leather. In Europe and Asia, flexible bags are the rule, but in America the rigid bag is king. Each type has advantages and drawbacks.

Rigid bags have limited capacity, and are in themselves heavy. However, rigid bags are strong, can be locked, and will offer some protection if you fall. The best argument in favor of rigid bags is that they are readily available in a wide range of styles and prices. You can usually find a set of bags to fit any bike and and any budget. The best argument against them is that they are often streamlined for esthetic reasons, making their interiors oddly shaped and thus reducing their effectiveness as storage units.

Flexible bags are inexpensive, can be stuffed full of odd gear, and weigh less than rigid bags. But they are prone to tearing off their mounts, are seldom weatherproof, and will not stop the determined thief. The leather variety of flexible saddlebag usually has a metal frame inside and mounts to the frame of the bike. These are flexible only in the sense that leather has more give than metal or fiber glass. The canvas bags usually have connecting straps and are draped across the back of the saddle.

On the whole, I advocate flexible bags, primarily for the added carrying capacity. It has been my experience that no matter how carefully I pack up, there is always something left over that must be jammed in somewhere. With rigid bags, this is seldom possible. But a soft bag always has room to grunt in that last pair of socks or the frying pan.

Since I am rigging an "ideal" bike, I will discuss the ideal side storage unit . . .

Backpacks. For maximum utilization of side storage space, exactly nothing beats two large, cheap backpacks. Backpacks usually come with compartmented interiors and a series of outside pockets. This allows the nomad to store high-priority items, like his first aid kit, and high-use items, such as weather gear, out where they can be reached without unpacking the whole bag. Buy cheap backpacks because they are made of canvas or heavy duck and are stronger than the light nylon "professional" models.

The backpacks are mounted on pack frames, and these in turn are mounted to your bike. $3 at the welder's will get this done, and $5 will get them mounted so as to be removable.

There are two necessary modifications, one to the backpacks, one to the frames. The backpacks must be waterproofed or you will wind up with soaked gear after the first shower you ride through. The pack frames must have supporting members welded across the bottoms to take the weight of the packs. This is because backpacks are designed to cope with the gentle up-and-down bounce of a hiker.

The repeated shocks of high-speed running will tear out the sockets that hold the packs on their frames.

Storage system prices: Luggage racks, $8 to $35.
Tank packs, $20 to $70.
Saddlebags, $40 to $100 for a set of rigids, $10 to $50 for a set of flexibles.
Backpacks and frames, $25 to $60 a set.

Information: Local bike dealers, sporting goods shops, Sources Appendix.

The ideally rigged road bike, then, will have a fairing, two mirrors, a set of pegs, handlebars, and saddle that produces maximum comfort for the rider, a small, sturdy luggage rack, a large tank pack, and a set of backpacks mounted over the rear axle. It will wear a set of road tires, new or in good condition.

Bear in mind that ideals are seldom achieved. If your budget prohibits rigging your bike to the ideal, spend what you have on safety first, comfort second, and carrying capacity last.

Wisdom

The Greenland Eskimo rigs his sled so that if it should break through the ice, his sealskin packet of dry clothes and dried food will go under last.

In 1877, the U.S. Army appointed a committee to find out why the Mescalero Apache kept winning against the cavalry. The committee's findings were that the Apache were more mobile, and that this was because they kept the weight their horses bore distributed better than the cavalry did.

The Bedouin allots one measure of time to readying himself for a journey, a measure to readying his camel, and three measures to loading the camel properly.

Ken Haldane, veteran of two round-the-world motorcycle trips, places proper rigging second in importance only to engine and tire maintenance in his daily inspections.

4.

CLOTHING

We assume at this point that you have your mount and that it is properly rigged for touring. The next step is to rig you. This means fitting you with the right clothing and protective gear for life on the road. In this chapter we'll deal with clothing.

Clothing includes everything you wear exclusive of helmet, boots and gloves, which are covered in the next chapter. We will approach the subject from the inside.

The nomad has a more intimate relationship with weather than his urban cousins. He therefore dresses for practicality rather than fashion. In this area, at least, the two-wheel nomad has a body of wisdom to fall back on, for travelers' clothing is one of the world's oldest technologies. There is good archaeological evidence to support the belief that Neolithic man understood the secret of keeping the climate next to his skin under control long before he understood the principles of house building or contained fire.

Layering

The technique of body-climate control is universal, which is demonstrated by the fact that all nomads utilize it, no matter what their geographic location. The Eskimo uses it, the Arab uses it, the Hun used it, and you can use it. It is called "layering."

Layering means choosing your clothing so that each item can be combined with every other item in such a way as to regulate the flow of air. The two physical principles involved are that still air insulates and that heat rises.

The Greenland Eskimo wears his hide clothing with the fur turned inside, which stills the air next to his body and conserves heat. His clothing is open at the bottom and closed at the top, allowing enough air to prevent perspiration and holding the warm air as it rises.

The desert Arab uses precisely the same system. He wears a light garment next to his skin to absorb moisture and a heavy one made of wool on the outside — wool because it radiates perspiration at a slow, controlled rate, cutting down on the body's water loss. His garments are loose to disperse heat in the day and drawn tight to conserve it at night.

This layering system, with variations, has been the mode for every nomadic culture of history, and all our modern technology has failed to improve on it.

Livingskins

Because he travels farther and faster than his predecessors, the motorcycle wanderer is subject to quicker changes of climate. It is not impossible to face snow and subzero weather, 95-degree deserts, and torrential rains all in the same day. I have done just that, running down from mile-high (and snowed-in) Prescott, Arizona, through the midday heat of Phoenix and into the rainy evening at Marfa, Texas.

As a result, the biker's clothing must not only be capable of handling the changes, but of doing so without undue work on the rider's part. This means that the basic layers, the underwear and surface clothing, have to be versatile in themselves. That is, they must be comfortable over a broad spectrum of conditions. This is accomplished by careful choice in fabric and design and by knowing what each piece of clothing is supposed to do.

Let's build an "ideal" bike nomad's wardrobe, from the inside out.

Underwear has the function of absorbing perspiration, of promoting comfort, and of controlling heat. For the first purpose, nothing is as good as cotton. Nylon or other synthetic underwear has a luxuriant feel, but not after you have sat on it all day. This is particularly important for members of the cloven sex because cotton underwear is somewhat out of fashion now. However, a small sacrifice of style will pay large dividends in comfort and absorption on the road.

Comfort is a matter of style, as far as men's underwear is concerned. Men's shorts come in either boxer — with legs — or brief — without legs — styles. Boxers have a tendency to bunch and wrinkle when you ride all day, and this induces discomfort. Anything that bunches will eventually chafe. Brief-style shorts have the added advantage of offering support for the genitals, thus keeping them off the saddle.

I have found that the ultimate short for bike riding is a pair of athlete's supportive briefs. They serve the same function as a jockey strap without putting those chafing bands across your buttocks.

You need three or four pairs, following the general rule for clothing: one on, one in the wash, and one or two clean.

Heat control with underwear can be accomplished two ways. You can purchase string-wear undershirts (which look like body-shaped fishnet) or full thermal underwear. Thermals, which come only in long-sleeve uppers and long-leg bottoms, are really warm on those cold, rainy days, but they will be too hot to wear on days that are only slightly cool. This means you will have to stop to take them off. String-wear offers a wider range of heat control because it is cool unless something is put over it. Thus, you can regulate the temperature with a string-wear undershirt by partially unbuttoning and rebuttoning the shirt worn over it.

My recommendation is string uppers, briefs, and a pair of thermal bottoms.

A final note for the ladies: whatever your views on Women's Lib, wear a bra when riding your bike. The constant jiggle of motorcycle riding produces a visually pleasant result in spectators but is hell on the participant. Even the less well endowed will be sore and discouraged at the end of a day's ride with unfettered breasts.

Socks should be of two sorts: heavy and light. You need a pair of light, comfortable socks next to your skin — these can be synthetics — and a pair of absorbent cotton or woolen ones outside those. If this seems a little fanatic, try it for a while and you will find it's the most comfortable and serviceable approach to footgloves.

You will need two sets of heavy socks and three or four of light. Keep each pair pinned together with a safety pin and you won't lose them in the wash. You can also pin them to your pant leg at night so you don't have to grope around in a cold, dark tent the next morning.

Next on the agenda is the day-to-day layer. This includes pants, shirts, and sweaters, and is the stuff you wear while riding, camping, and truckin' around town.

Pants need to be long in the leg, to fit over your boot tops while riding, loose in the crotch, to keep from binding, and comfortable at the waist. They should be of a sturdy material, easily cared for, and fashionable enough for the lifestyle you intend to lead.

I have found that permanent-press jeans in fashionable patterns work best. They can be worn in camp, on the bike, and around town with equal ease, and can be tossed in a washer/dryer and worn immediately. Further, they are available almost anywhere, and in both men's and women's styles. With a jacket and tie, I have worn such pants to the opera, into fine restaurants, and even to a reception for an out-of-work king. Only once did I incur hostility, and a superior sneer on my part squelched that.

Since we are building an "ideal" wardrobe, let's put in it three pairs of pants: two jeans and one pair of slacks, all permanent press.

Shirts are almost useless to the nomad. They have collars that flap and flay your neck, cuffs that pop buttons and catch on things, and waists that bunch and ride. But I wear them, just like everybody else. My recommendation is two shirts with button-down collars, long-sleeved, and loose at the waist. Permanent press, of course.

Incidentally, with the price of clothing what it is today, you might consider learning the basic nomadic skill of sewing. It is simpler than either carpentry or welding, takes minimal equipment, and can save you fortunes. A dress shirt that costs $10 in the store can be made for under $4. If you can build a shirt, you can build a tent, or a sleeping bag, or any number of other costly items. I have been sewing my own gear for three years and figure that I have saved somewhere in the neighborhood of $1,000 by doing so. If you do not already own this basic skill, any competent person would be happy to show a dashing adventurer how to do it.

Sweaters. The most important items in the day-to-day layer of your clothing are sweaters. That's plural because you need two of them.

You need, first, a light, neckless sweater with long sleeves. Preferably something made of wool. This garment will keep you cool in the heat and warm in the cold. It can be worn over your string underwear for one temperature, over your shirt for another, and over both for still another. It is the perfect garment for sitting around the campfire in the evening while cooking supper and recounting your many exploits to the lucky friend with you. This sweater should be of fine quality, for the good ones hold their shape longer and will wear almost indefinitely. It should be light in color, as it will reflect heat and keep you cool.

I once rode across the waste between Desert Center and Indio, California, with the noontime temperature standing at 126 degrees. I tried every combination of upper garments from my jacket to my bare skin and found that my light sweater kept me coolest. It provided just the right balance between evaporation and heat absorption.

Your second sweater should be a big, bulky cable-knit of the Irish variety. These things are fantastic in the chill night, and absolutely indispensable when it gets really cold. This garment should have a high neck and good, long sleeves. Again, buy the best you can afford.

Sweaters complete the day-to-day, or livingskins, portion of your wardrobe. We now come to the outer layer, whose purpose is to protect you no matter how inclement the climate. This layer is called weatherskins.

Weatherskins

This includes all garments worn over your livingskins. There are many approaches to this final layer, so let's look at it in some depth.

Leather is the most common approach to weatherskins. The leather jacket — and pants, for that matter — is almost symbolic of the motorcyclist, and there are some good reasons why. No woven fabric has the tensile strength of leather. Few fabrics are as windproof. Few fabrics are as easily waterproofed or cared for as leather. There are

Types of weatherskins: leather, down-filled nylon (ski suit), and specially treated fabric riding suits.

more leather garments made strictly for the motorcyclist than any other piece of equipment.

Leather, however, has some drawbacks. It is expensive, running from $35 to $150 a garment. It is not intrinsically warm, which is why leather jackets have linings. And leather garments, no matter how well cut, are not as comfortable as fabric.

Leather's prime failing, though, is that it is heavy and bulky. For the nomad who travels on two wheels, these are serious considerations. The amount of space on a motorcycle is limited, and so is the weight-bearing capacity. Leather garments, particularly if lined, are clumsy items to store and take up an amount of space disproportionate to the service they render you.

But a lot of nomads swear by leather, and if you feel

you have the space and weight margin to carry it, you might consider it.

The riding suit is the second approach, and also a popular one. A riding suit is an all-weather garment, usually one piece, which is designed specifically for the biker. It is made of fabric and treated in various ways to make it waterproof.

The advantages of riding suits are in fit and suitability. Since they are designed for bike riding, they tend to fit better than anything else, and thus be more comfortable. The better ones have auxiliary features worth their weight in gold: pockets that can be opened and closed one-handed and with gloves on, collars that keep the rain out, vents to let the heat out, etc. There is also a certain snob value in having a riding suit, since most of them look like they were designed for something furtive and romantic.

The disadvantages of riding suits are, first, they are nearly as expensive as leather, costing from $60 up for a complete outfit; second, they are also bulky and noncompactible; third, they tend to be uncomfortable to wear in warm, moist situations, such as Mexican summer rains; finally, the compounds used to waterproof them all rub off on your livingskins. The best of the bunch, made by an English firm called Barbours', are coated with a black goo that leaves sooty smudges on the collars of your shirts and the cuffs of your pants.

But they *do* keep you dry and warm, and if you don't mind looking as though you've been standing downwind of the campfire, you should think about a riding suit.

Ski gear and rainsuits form the last approach to weather-skins. This is the method I have come to use after trying leather and riding suits, and I have found nothing better in the last four years. By ski gear I mean the down-filled nylon jackets and pants made for skiers.

The advantages of ski gear are light weight and compressibility, versatility in climate control, correctness of design, and a couple of odd factors I'll cover in a moment.

A ski jacket, even a heavy one, is weighed in ounces. Riding suits and leather jackets are weighed in pounds. As far as weatherskins are concerned, nothing is as light as ski gear. This matter of weight is not as picayune as it sounds. Remember that you have something under 200 pounds to work with, and in that measure you must fit your *entire* traveling home, tent, kitchen, clothing, tools, and all. A saving of 2 pounds will make a tremendous difference in what you can take or leave behind, and a saving of 10 pounds will have a demonstrable effect on the handling of your mount. Colin Fletcher, the complete walker, speaks of backpackers who cut the strings off their tea bags to save weight and space. I know of a number of bikers who perform similar surgery on their equipment for the same reasons. I use a toothbrush that contains its own toothpaste, simply to conserve space and weight. These measures seem absurd only to the uninitiated.

The down-filled jacket is comfortable over a larger range of weather conditions than any other garment. Because it can be zippered from both the bottom and top and can be cinched or left open at the waist, it offers tremendous control over the flow of air. When snugged tight, a down jacket will keep you warm in 30-degree cold. When opened up, it will keep you cooler than a shirt.

Down pants have the same characteristics as the jackets, with the added attraction of usually having a bootstrap to keep them down where they belong when the wind howls.

I have never worn down pants because I seldom ride in desperately cold weather and because I think I look good with blue legs and frozen toes, but the folks who use them say they are superb.

The odd factors I mentioned before are these: ski gear is available in a number of high-visibility colors (not yellow, for instance, but YELLOW!), which helps the drunks spot you, and it is useful in camp. A balled-up ski jacket makes the best pillow you can find, perfect for leaning against in your sleeping bag while reading Kafka or Sartre. Ski gear can be stuffed into the bag with you and will be nice and warm to put on when nature calls at four A.M. You will appreciate this if you have ever crawled into an icy leather jacket under the same circumstances.

The disadvantages of down-filled weatherskins are expense — they also cost fortunes — fragility, and lack of waterproofing.

A down jacket costs from $35 to $80, with pants in about the same range. You can get them cheaper, but you will be wasting your money. Again, never scrimp on survival tools.

Nylon and goose feathers are not a durable combination. A good riding suit will last you five or six years, given reasonable care. A good leather garment is practically indestructible. But a ski jacket, if you use it regularly, will wear out in two to three years. When you figure the frequency of replacement into the cost of your weatherskins, this is an expensive way to go. Remember, too, that if you ever go down, you might as well have tissue paper between you and the concrete.

The final disadvantage is lack of waterproofing. You *can* waterproof nylon, but that is a sealing process that leaves you on the inside, neatly packaged behind the seal and a lot of very efficient down. A good way to lose weight without dieting.

To get around this problem, carry a rainsuit. Rainsuits come in heavy, rubberized models, which are expensive and wear like cast iron, and in cheap plastic models, which fall apart when you breathe on them. I use the latter kind.

The heavy-duty rainsuits have the disadvantages of leather and other waterproofed fabrics: bulk and weight.

You don't wear a rainsuit much, and all the time you aren't wearing it you have to store it.

The plastic suits are good only for three or four wearings, but they weigh nothing and can be folded into a small package that will stuff anywhere. I keep mine in one of my fairing pockets, where it is handy and still out of the way.

A light rainsuit worn over a ski jacket keeps you comfortable in the cold rain and snow and, worn over your sweater, keeps you comfortable in the warm rain. It also makes the perfect windbreaker over anything, adding the final coating to your weatherskins system.

The only problem with rainsuits, particularly the plastic ones, is ecological. They wear out rapidly and there is *nothing* you can do with the remains that doesn't pollute. You can't burn or bury them, and chopping them up just makes a lot of little problems. I usually dump mine in the trash as I pass through a city and try not to look guilty. I also avoid remembering when I was the ecology editor of the Los Angeles *Free Press*.

In the balance, then, weatherskins options are leather, which is durable, protective, and waterproof; riding suits, which are comfortable, correctly designed, and also waterproof; and ski gear, which is climatically versatile, light and compactible, and has odd uses when you're off the bike. Each system has its advantages and disadvantages, and each has its advocates. All are expensive, though you can beat this with ski gear by making your own. (Kit manufacturers can be found in the Sources Appendix.)

There is a last, strange advantage to wearing fragile nylon ski wear. Owning leather weatherskins or heavy riding suits has much the same psychological effect as buying a new bike: it puts your head on sideways. For some reason, a person who is zipped and buttoned into a leather suit seems to feel as though he is armor-plated. He will take risks and do maneuvers he would consider insane in another rider. But it is good to remember that no mail-coated Knight Errant ever collided with a Buick at a combined velocity of 140 mph.

A nice, flimsy nylon weatherskin will do wonders for your "bravery" when you think about passing that camper on a curve.

If it seems that I advocate timidity, you're right. It's the prime survival factor on the highways. I have faced — successfully — bears, fires, hurricanes, armed husbands, and the Viet Cong, and I tell you that none of them are as dangerous as the average mile of public highway. Remember that you can't impress the beach bunnies with your prowess if you aren't there.

What to Look for in Weatherskins

Whatever approach to weatherskins you adopt, there are certain things to look for in them.

Construction of the garment is first. Look for well-sewn seams, with even stitching and no loose threads. Look for French seams at the major joints (sleeve-to-body, side seams, etc.). If a garment doesn't have this type of seam it doesn't mean it is a bad garment, only that it isn't built to the ultimate.

Look for sturdy closures, zippers and buttons of the heavy-duty variety. Check for workability. Could you manipulate them at night in the rain without their tearing?

Fit is tricky. A garment that looks and feels fine while leaning against the bar or admiring yourself in the mirror might be a disaster on your mount. Be sure to test the fit of your garment sitting down, preferably with your motorcycle under you.

Look for sufficient length in the arms and legs to keep the weatherskins over your wrists and boot tops. Bear in mind that much of your riding will be done in a semi-crouch, and that this position pulls legs and arms out of line in clothing.

In jackets, look for a tail that will stay down when you ride. Long coats without split tails will strangle you when you button them up. Those with split tails will flap unless you sit on them — an uncomfortable procedure. The ideal is a rump-length jacket that will just brush the saddle when you sit. The waist-length jackets will balloon when the wind sucks at your back.

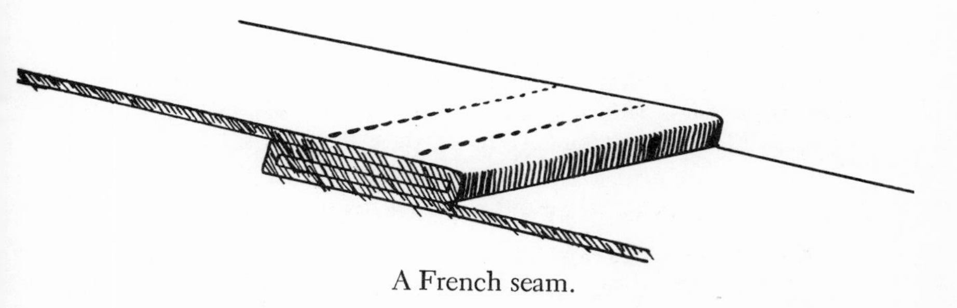

A French seam.

In pants, look for roomy crotches, instep straps if possible, and correctly built front zippers. Correct in this case means weatherproof. A crotch design that will allow rain to seep in will make your pants worthless.

If you follow the ski gear and rainsuit approach, look for rainpants with a high, bib front and no crotch opening at all. If you have to get them off fast, you'll find a way.

Collars on your jacket should be of the mandarin variety and should close all the way up. Make sure you get yours big enough in diameter to wear over your thick sweater. If you can't get a mandarin collar, at least get one that closes snugly enough to keep out the worst of the weather.

Cuffs on the jacket should be either elastic or strap. Elastic cuffs fit better than strap closures, but they offer little protection at the wrist. Strap closures — and the snap type — are a little clumsy, but they place a lot more material between you and the environment than an elastic cuff. Your choice is comfort or protection.

Cuffs on pants can be either kind without much sacrifice in comfort or protection. The cuffs of your pants will usually be inside your boots, over your socks, and under your weatherskin pants, so there is adequate protection in any case.

There are a couple of accessories you might think about. One is a scarf. I do not use one myself but have often wished I did. I'm told that scarves have a lot of uses around camp and that they are nice social accessories. Personally, I think they take up too much room on the bike.

I carry a balaclava helmet, which is a knitted skiers' mask that covers your head and face, with holes for your nose and eyes. I wear it on cold evenings in camp with the bottom half rolled up to make a watch cap. I have worn it down a couple of times while riding in extreme cold and found that it keeps my cheeks warm but does nothing for my nose. It also collects breath moisture and ices up, enabling me to frighten small children when I pull in for gas.

This completes the weatherskins and livingskins portions of your nomadic wardrobe. There remains the social.

If you have chosen well in your livingskins, coordinating colors and fabrics, you should need nothing more than a coat and tie. If your tastes don't include the opera or an occasional high-priced meal, you can get along quite well without either. I carry a jacket and tie simply to dress up every now and then.

For the lady nomad the problem is a little harder. You need not only a dress or suit, but all the accouterments, and that can take up both space and weight. There is almost no way you can wear a dress while riding or in camp. It's not only uncomfortable and impractical, but downright dangerous. I once watched a lady swing her dress through a Coleman stove's flame and set fire to her fanny. Another lady, with whom I traveled for a while, laid her damp rayon blouse over her still-warm engine to dry it after a swim. She wound up with the only paisley BSA for miles around.

The best solution I've seen to this problem belonged to a girl from Kentucky. She adopted a Country Slicker pastiche of jeans and checked blouses, which allowed her an elegant simplicity of dress and adornment, utilizing one pair of earrings, some almost-flat shoes, and a nice, easily stored knit handbag.

The qualities you seek in your wardrobe are durability, suitability to purpose, ease of care and cleaning, and compactibility.

Good brands, price ranges, and further information can be found through the Sources Appendix.

Wisdom

Plastic Baggies worn over the socks and inside the boots will keep your feet dry in a flood.

A catalytic pocket warmer in the jacket pocket will warm you 10 degrees.

"He travels best who dresses lightest"

— *Arapahoe saying*

"The wise traveler dresses for tomorrow's weather"

— *Beni Faquat saying*

5.
GLOVES, BOOTS, AND HELMETS

The head, the hands, and the feet are your body's most active parts. They are also the most easily damaged. They freeze first in the cold, blister first in the heat, and break first in an accident. This chapter deals with protecting them, and it starts with your hands.

Gloves

Gloves are inefficient devices. If they are thick enough to keep your fingers warm, they are usually too bulky to work in. If they are thin and flexible, they seldom offer much protection.

Fortunately, there is a way around this problem: buy two pairs.

Your first pair should be of the knit sort, with long wrists and fully articulated fingers. Wear this pair when in camp. It allows you maximum use of your hands, and that usage will help keep your fingers warm. The long wrists are for insulation. The cuffs of any jacket are its weakest point of insulation because there is direct contact there from skin to fabric to blizzard, and anything you can use to cover your wrist — like a nice woolen glove — will be a blessing.

The best woolen gloves around are the U.S. Army ones, available for about a dollar at any surplus store.

Your second pair of gloves should be leather bikers' gauntlets. These come in either articulated or mitten styles. If possible, get the mittens. When you isolate each finger in its own little wrapper, you are just presenting more surface to the cold. A mitten produces a dead-air space enclosing all your fingers and is anywhere from 15 to 60 percent warmer than an articulated glove.

"Gauntlet" refers to wrist construction. A gauntlet has an apron that comes well up the arm to keep the wind and rain off your wrists. In your gauntlets, you *do not* want wrist closures. The purpose of this outer layer is deflection, not heat conservation.

When you are riding, your hands are fairly static. When they are used, the motions are seldom delicate. You can pull back a clutch lever just as well with mittens as with articulated gloves, so pass up the flashy skiers' and bikers' gloves with the racing stripes down the thumbs and buy the ugly, functional mittens.

Separately and in combination, a pair of woolen inner gloves and a pair of leather mittens will handle almost any combination of weather you are likely to encounter. If you are tempted to get some nice, soft chamois or kid inner gloves, don't. When it gets too cold in camp to wear your woolies, you aren't likely to be picking guitar or doing brain surgery, and your mittens will do nicely. And bear in mind that inclement weather is often wet weather, and that kid and chamois take a very, very long time to dry out.

In gloves, seek strong construction at the thumb seam, in woolies, even knitting, in both pairs, long wrists and proper fit. The fit of your woolens should be snug, and the fit of your mittens should be fairly loose. Remember the Eskimo principle: allow air to circulate but control its flow.

Some bikers' mittens come with extra-thick leather on the palms because you instinctively stick your hand out if you get unlucky. If you can't find gloves with this feature, make it a point not to fall down.

Boots and Footgloves

Boots and footgloves are prime tools. They do more work than any other piece of your weatherskins, and under more adverse conditions. When it is raining on your jacket, it's usually slopping all over your boots.

You need two or three sets of footwear, depending on your social life. You need main boots, a pair of footgloves for camp, and perhaps some dress shoes for around town. You can avoid the third pair if you choose your main boots with some care.

Main boots are those you wear while riding and while working off your mount. You wear them while setting up camp, while tromping through the underbrush, and while running from bears. In short, you wear them for everything except relaxing and socializing.

Main boots need to be several things at once: comfortable, rugged, easily maintained, handsome — if you're to use them for city truckin'— and most of all, correctly built. For those unfamiliar with their feet, this may seem simple, but it isn't. Boot construction is a complex thing, and few bootmakers manage to get it all together in one design.

The perfect pair of main boots will have high tops — one piece if possible — heel-supporting molded counters, steel-reinforced shanks, sweat-resistant insoles, heavy-duty midsoles, waterproof tongue or closure construction, full-cut heels, tough outsoles, a leather heel guard, good arch and ankle support, and a sole design that gives firm grip on any terrain.

Obviously, you aren't going to find many that meet all

these requirements and are still comfortable and handsome. However, there are some. Since boots, like bike fairings, are an arcane subject to most folks, I'll examine a few here for you.

The cheapest "good" boot available is a pair of army jungle boots from the Viet Nam fiasco. They can be gotten for between $10 and $18 in a surplus store, and for far less than that used. These boots have canvas and leather uppers and spike-proof Vibram soles, which is useful if you plan on invading somebody. They fit well, are surprisingly well-constructed for government contract work, and are positively the toughest boots in the known universe. I imagine that somebody somewhere has worn a pair of these things out, but I don't know about it.

The disadvantage of these boots is the canvas portion of the uppers. The stuff cannot really be waterproofed without making it uncomfortable and smelly, and it offers little protection from snakes, although that's a highly overrated danger in the United States. Still, they are the cheapest main boots you can get that will function correctly.

The West Coast Shoe Company makes a superboot for loggers and foresters that is superb for the bike nomad. It's called the 210V and costs about $32. It has Vibram soles with the best lug pattern I've yet seen on a boot. These things will give you traction on greased marbles. The 210V features an undercut heel design that allows you to step correctly, distributing stress through the center of the ankle. It's a lace-up and has a waterproof tongue design. My gripe with the 210V is that it's ugly. It was designed for pure function and looks it. It's great to climb mountains in, but looks kind of silly in the Stork Club.

White's Shoe Shop offers a line of serious boots for serious business and will custom build for you — a service that's getting hard to obtain. Their gear is expensive, running above $50, but worth the price. They use fine, fine leather — brown elk, black kip, etc. If you like an old-fashioned boot, built to old-fashioned standards, these are the people to see.

There are boots designed for bikers, and the best of these are made by Chippewa. They build an engineer-style pull-on that has *all* the features I detailed earlier. They come like Henry Ford's Model T — in black or black, and in prices from $28.95 to $55. If you like the Marlon Brando image or simply want an excellently designed and built boot, you need to consider these.

My personal choice is a ridiculously expensive boot made by a firm called Gokey, up in Minnesota. It's called the Gokey Botte Sauvage and it's mostly handmade. It has a one-piece upper 9½ inches high, an adjustable instep strap, and a top closure buckle. I have found this boot to be strong, comfortable, durable, and equally at home on rocks or city streets. It comes in brown or black, takes shoe polish well, and is handsomely cut. It is not out of place when worn with a suit and tie. The Botte Sauvage runs $55 and is available in men's and women's models.

There is a peculiar demand made on a biker's boots. They tend to wear in odd places because they are used for shifting gears. If your bike has its gearshift lever on the left side, your left boot will soon wear a shiny spot on top of the left upper.

The soles will wear fairly quickly, too, due to the tendency of the rider to put his feet down when stopping. This scuffing will wear out a boot faster than you would think, and you need to keep this in mind when buying your main boots.

Don't be silly enough to put steel taps on your boots. That's a sure way to wind up being laughed at as you lie at the stoplight with five hundred pounds of bike and gear on top of you. I can personally testify that this is one of the least impressive positions the nomad can assume.

The argument against wearing shoes instead of boots is just that shoes are poor protection against weather or stones. For your main footwear, you *must* wear boots.

Around camp, however, wear footgloves.

Footgloves are the softest, most comfortable things you can find to put on your feet. Wear them in your tent, when sitting around the fire, and when walking on soft ground. Their function is to make you feel good, not to protect.

Footgloves are a personal matter. I've seen people who wore loafers, people who wore tennis shoes, and people who wore moccasins. The general rule is: whatever feels good to you.

Moccasins are a good bet, though, because they are light and compactible and can be stored very easily. Being leather, they do offer protection, though it's minor.

Myself, I wear a pair of rubber shower shoes. These things are completely useless from a protection standpoint — particularly when you step in an anthill — but I like them and they're only 49¢ a pair.

There is a kind of combination shoe/sock backpackers wear that you might consider. They are down-filled, quilted affairs with slightly reinforced soles. Colin Fletcher says they are warm and comfortable, and they can be jammed into a space the size of a saltshaker or something. They also cost about $8, which seems steep to me.

Finally, *social shoes*. Again, a matter of taste. But remember that dress shoes are clumsy to store, take some care, and are of limited use to the nomad. For the lady they are almost a necessity since no boot made will look too chic with an evening gown, but men might well dispense with them.

I have to admit that until I got my Sauvages, I carried dress shoes. And I always managed to find a place to store them when riding.

Helmets

Helmets are a sore subject in this country. There are states that require you to wear them, which is unconstitutional, and states which don't, which is idiotic. I cannot in good conscience support a law designed to protect me from myself. And there is no real difference between a mandatory helmet law and a law requiring seat belts on rocking chairs.

But neither can I help but sympathize with the thinking behind such laws. Anyone who would ride without a helmet has to be out of his mind.

Consider for a moment the functions centered in your skull. It is the repository of all your data, the center of your decision-making processes, the control center of your very existence. And all that in a fragile little ball balanced on a few vertebrae.

The simple fact is that if you bash up your skull, the whole show is over. Here are a couple of gruesome statistics: 90 percent of all motorcycle accidents occur in the first week of ownership of a bike; 78 percent of all motorcycle fatalities are caused by head injuries; 89 percent of all those fatal head injuries happen to people who aren't wearing helmets. That first statistic argues well for a rider education program in this country. The second proves the point I made in the last paragraph. The third speaks for itself.

But like a lot of problems, there are no simple solutions for the uninitiated. Helmets all look alike from the outside, and you cannot go by price.

Inside, helmets differ vastly.

The basic controversy is over the material used in constructing helmet shells. The two common materials are polyurethane and fiber glass. Each has its proponents, and each its detractors. The pro-poly element cites greater impact resistance and less wear. The pro-fiber element offers proof of greater penetration resistance and of less damage due to chemical changes. The fact is that a well-constructed helmet made of either material will give you good protection, and a poorly made one will kill you. My preference is fiber glass as far as shell materials go, but it is a prejudice, not a knowledge of superiority.

As in most high-technology items, the buyer must depend on brand name and on impartial testing to prove the worth of the product. In helmets, that means you stick with the better-known brands, and the better models of each brand. As for impartial testing, there are two helmet certification agencies in the United States. One is called the Z-90, the other the Snell Foundation. The Snell Foundation was formed in the late 1950s after an amateur sports-car racer named Pete Snell died in a wreck because of helmet failure. It's a nonprofit organization that can't be bought for love or money and has test standards several times higher than the Z-90's. Almost any helmet you can buy will pass a Z-90 test and will say so on the sticker. But only the best pass the Snell tests, and they are the ones to look for. Mind you, any helmet is better than no helmet, but there's an old saw that goes, "If you have a $10 head, get a $10 helmet." Good helmets cost from $30 to $80, and are worth it.

Helmets come in degrees of coverage, from "shorty" styles that are really hard hats with chin straps to "magnum" styles, which are those astronaut thingees with the hole carved in the front. In choosing your helmet, pick a style that is most comfortable for you. The general rule is: the more coverage the better. However, magnums cut down on both vision and hearing, which can be important, and they are heavy. A well-made helmet will have some degree of balance, but the more coverage you have the more weight your neck has to support.

Look for sufficient padding inside to keep the lid off your head while still fitting snugly. Check carefully for comfort around the ears, and for any tendency to slip down over your face when you shake your head. Look for visor snaps and for a comfortable and easy-to-operate chin strap.

Your helmet should be just a little snug when new because it will fit correctly after a few wearings. Snug, not tight. The usual "give" in a new helmet is about one head size.

Good brands: Bell, Grant, Akia, Honda.

6.
SHELTER

The basic component of your traveling home is your "house" itself. Since you will spend as much time in it as you will on the road, it deserves thorough consideration.

Tents, Near-Tents, and No Tents

The limits of the two-wheel nomad's house are defined by the carrying capacity of his mount, which is why that house must be made of fabric. Fabric houses fall into two groups, tents and near-tents. There is a third option, no tent at all, which I'll talk about later.

A tent is a complete enclosure, providing shelter over, under, and around you. Its job is to control the flow of moisture and to separate you from the bugs. A near-tent is a rain fly or tarpaulin, an open shelter without a floor. Its job is to keep rain off you and to break the force of the wind. Both types of shelter will keep you dry when rigged properly; tents will keep insects away, and near-tents will control moisture better. Neither shelter will keep you warm — that's a function of your sleeping bag and a gadget I'll talk about later.

Tents come in either nylon or cotton, and in treated and untreated versions. "Treated" means waterproofed with a gunk of some sort. Untreated material is better, because treating closes the tent's pores and leads to condensation. Condensation occurs when your tent is sealed at night and when it rains. Your body throws off nearly a pint of moisture while you sleep, and if your tent doesn't breathe, that moisture will settle like the dew all over you and everything in your house. When it rains, the cooler air outside will condense moisture inside your home with the same effect.

Therefore, avoid treated materials if possible.

Cotton tents come in twills, duck, and poplins. The best is "army duck," which has a high thread count per square inch. Since cotton waterproofs itself by the swelling of the threads, the higher the count, the drier the tent. A good thread count is 200 and above. However, when those threads swell, they have the same effect as treating the fabric: they close up and invite condensation.

The prime disadvantage of cotton tents is their bulk. You can get a lot more tent space in nylon than in cotton for the same weight and space penalty. This is not as acute a problem for the motorcycle nomad as for a backpacker or a bicyclist, but it does rule out the big family-type tents that the car freaks carry around, unless you are traveling with another biker and can share the load.

A moisture-control problem with untreated tents — both nylon and cotton — is capillary action. Touch the tent wall when it's wet and it leaks. If you have a large tent this is seldom a real problem. But if you have a small one, where you must stack gear against the walls or where you will brush against them, it is a very real thing.

The solution to both problems, condensation and capillary action, is to have a double-wall tent. This is a tent within a tent and consists of your tent itself and a fly sheet over it, usually about four or five inches from the tent walls. The fly sheet can be waterproofed nylon or plastic, and the tent can be anything that breathes. The fly sheet keeps the wet off the tent, and the tent keeps the bugs off you.

Tents come with a mind-boggling array of options, gadgets, and special features, most of which you don't need. The things you do need are: sewn-in, waterproof floor, ventilating flaps that can be left open in the rain far enough to allow moisture to escape, sewn-in bug screens on the windows and doors, strong seams and tie-down points, comfortable color. This last point bears examination. Remember that you have to live inside your tent, and if it happens to be hot pink, you'll be living in a hot pink bowl. Best colors are tan, burnt orange, soft yellows and light blue.

Look for a tent that can be set up swiftly and securely, because you will eventually have to do it in the dark and the rain.

Tent brands. There are many, many tents around. Here are some of the better ones.

Bishop's are expensive, professional tents made for the serious explorer. They're designed by Barry Bishop, who has stood on top of Mt. Everest. Lots of models available, all good.

Black's is an old British firm that builds stiff-upper-lip tents. Their tents are heavy, thoughtfully designed, and rugged as hell.

Eureka Tent and Awning makes stuff for the car campers, all of which is useless to the bike nomad, and a number of tents, which do very well. Their gear is not the best made, but the economy backpackers' line is genuinely cheap. If you're counting change, Eureka is a good bet.

Draw-Tite, sometimes known as Alpine Draw-Tite, makes tents for the rich folks. They are overpriced and heavy, but they work well and offer a lot of interior room because of their unique frame design. This same design frees them from being pegged down, and you can just pick one up and move it to higher ground if you have to without breaking the whole thing down.

Gerry produces the best-thought-out tents around, then charges you for all that excellence. I have used a couple of their tents and can honestly say that if I weren't such a cheapskate, I'd buy one for myself.

Poptent is a sort of fabric dome made by Thermos and is probably the best tent there is from a biker's viewpoint. It comes in two sizes (6½ feet and 8½ feet floor diagonals) and with an external frame. The smaller one weighs about 13 pounds, and the larger about 19 pounds. Both fit on a motorcycle very easily and set up quickly. These tents have good wind stability. The smaller one will stand up to a fairly healthy hurricane without taking off across the swamp.

My own tent is a big cotton affair made by Black's. It's a four-man Scottish mountain tent that measures 6 by 7 feet on the floor and has nearly 7 feet of headroom. It can be rigged with an internal "T" pole or external lines, has nylon bug netting, a reinforced plastic floor, a flap over the rear window, and a rainproof moisture vent near the roof. The thing is bigger and heavier than anything I would recommend for anyone else, but I like a lot of elbow room and Ganesh hasn't complained about the burden yet. I have used this house for two hard years and it shows zero wear.

Tents cost $35 to $300.

Information: other tenters, the Sources Appendix, everybody's catalogues.

Near tents have the advantages of light weight and compactibility, of versatility, and of putting you closer to your environment. A tarpaulin with grommets and ties in strategic places can be rigged more ways than a small-town election. It can also be set up in a real hurry, which many tents cannot. And a tarp or fly sheet will cost you a lot less than the cheapest usable tent.

Since a near-tent is just a wind and rain break, it has

none of the moisture-control problems that an enclosed tent has. It *will* allow natural dew to collect on you if it isn't rigged correctly, but this is less annoying than waking up bathed in your own sweat.

The drawback with near-tents is that they do not keep your inquisitive six-legged friends at bay. In the three years that I used a near-tent, I had every sort of visitor from sand fleas to scorpions crawl in with me. Granted, they didn't take up that much space, but they were all pushy in one way or another.

No tents. The last approach to shelter is none at all. Don't discard this idea without thinking about it.

Having no tent or fly makes you more resourceful. It will make you learn to deal with the earth on its own terms, and that is a good thing. In this country we are blessed with the most consistently temperate climate on the earth. There is no other land where you can cover so much ground and still be in a gentle climate. Remember that man is an animal designed for bare-handed survival. It is only living in cities that has deprived him of his confidence in his body's resilience.

How to Determine Your Shelter Needs

Esthetic consideration aside, there are practical ways to determine the best shelter system for yourself. How much shelter you need depends on how long you will be traveling, how much you will camp, and what season you will pass through. Time, the first factor, is a measure of your chances of meeting inclement weather. If you are going down the road only for a week or so, and the forecast is good, you can get away with nothing. A longer trip means possible rain. A very long trip means certain rain, sooner or later. Extended rain means you must have enough shelter to carry on daily functions like cooking and eating without getting soaked.

How much you camp dictates shelter needs in that a long camp will cause you to accumulate things in and around your shelter, necessitating more protected room.

And travel in the winter, or in a wet spring, makes a full tent almost mandatory. When choosing your shelter, bear in mind that you may be confined to it for as long as a week in really awful weather.

The intersection of time and weather, coupled with your own needs in shelter, forms another three-vector system. Rate your shelter needs from minimal to maximal in all three vectors, then find the area where they all coincide. A long trip in the summer for a person who likes to get close to the ground, for example, calls for a fly sheet or near-tent. That same trip for someone who wants to keep the bugs off demands a tent. Tent for a short trip in the winter; nothing for a trip in the spring, provided the forecast is good; near-tent for an overnight run up to Sausalito, even in the chill.

The other half of your shelter system is your sleeping bag. It provides the warmth in your house and, more than you would expect, the comfort. You will find that you spend almost as much time sitting on your bag as you do sleeping in it.

Sleeping Bags: Types and Functions

The purpose of your sleeping bag is to give you a comfortable night's rest, to keep you warm, and to control moisture flow. There is no bag made that will give you the maximum effect on all three. Comfort is a function of shape, warmth of material, and moisture control of construction.

Comfort depends on how much you thrash around at night. Sleeping bags come in two basic styles. The first is called "mummy," the second "rectangular" or "open."

Mummy bags fit your body and zip up so that only your nose is out in the cold air. They are designed for maximum heat conservation. If you are a log-sawer, you will find these bags comfortable and easy to live with. But if you move around a lot or plan to take a compatible friend with you, the mummy-style bag will be a chore. You can't get very social in a mummy bag unless one of you is a contortionist.

Open bags are like two blankets sewn together. They are designed for boy scouts and mild climates. They usually zip up the side and have an open top. They are less warm than mummies but offer much more elbow room. Most of the better models can be zipped together with another to form a two-person bedroll.

I have found that aside from basic warmth, the most important comfort factor in a sleeping bag is its suitability to your particular sleeping style. If you're a tumbler, don't even consider a mummy. If you're a sound sleeper, don't bother with an open bag.

Warmth is obtained by the material from which your bag is built. The best material is goose down, which I discussed in the weatherskins section. Here is why it's best: No material used in clothing or bag construction is warm in itself. The warmth is your own, *conserved* by the garment or bag. In fact, it is the dead-air space between your body and the bag that keeps you warm, not the material in the bag. Any material that will keep a dead-air space next to your body will keep you warm, including a pile of leaves or a cocoon of glazed snow.

Down is the most effective insulating material, so that you need less down than anything else to keep that air near you. Down has a lot of other good features, including great compressibility and light weight. There are other materials used. In decreasing effectiveness, they are: polyester fiber, acetate fiber, wool, and cotton. As the effectiveness of the insulator goes down, the weight and bulk of the bag go up. Conversely, though, the price usually goes down, with down-filled bags being the most expensive and cotton ones the cheapest.

When choosing your bag, take a realistic look at the weather you are likely to encounter. Do you really need the Tenzing Norgay Everest Special? Perhaps you can get away with a wool bag. I am not advocating cutting any necessary corners. Your bag is the second most important item in your touring system, right behind your mount. But do assess your needs accurately. You can save a mint by moving from down to polyester fiber.

Moisture flow is governed partially by the material used — down again being the best — but mostly by the way the bag is constructed. The problem with loose fillers is that they shift around inside the bag's walls. To prevent this, bags are stitched in various patterns, forming pockets to contain the filler. These pockets are called baffles, and baffle design is a whole, weird little world of its own. Ultimately, the more baffles you put in a bag, the better the distribution of the filler. But also, the heavier the bag and the more bulk.

Basically, bags are laid out in channels, into which are sewn box pockets. The type of pocket in the channels is not as important as the direction the channels take relative to the bag itself. The least effective channels are longitudinal, since they allow a gradual shift of the filler to your feet. Next best is transverse channeling, which runs across the bag, and best of all is chevron channeling, which is sewn in a series of "V's" with the points toward your toes.

Moisture flow is controlled by the osmosis of perspiration through the bag. If your bag has badly designed channels and pockets, that flow will be retarded and you will get damp and uncomfortable.

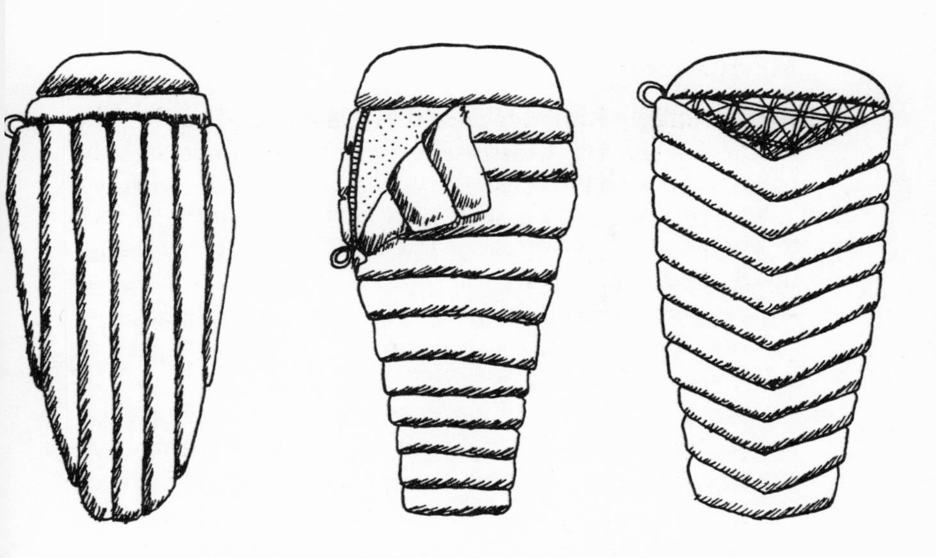

Sleeping-bag channeling: longitudinal, transverse, and chevron.

Some bags, like tents, are waterproofed. And, again like tents, this is to be avoided.

What price comfort? Sleeping bags cost from $10 for the real cheapos to $120 for the supers. Where do you start looking?

First off, do not compromise on your needs. If you feel you truly need a down-filled bag, *get* a down-filled bag. If not, move down the list of materials until you find what you need.

Second, consider again the twin banes of the two-wheel nomad: weight and space. The cotton and wool bags can get awfully heavy and form gargantuan lumps to have to strap on your bike. If you save a nickel on your bag, will you lose it in the storage? Remember that cotton and wool absorb water, and that a wet bag can pick up as much as 6 pounds of moisture.

Finally, buy the very best model you can afford, whatever type and material bag you choose. It's best not to start out with a sum and find a bag to fit it. Find the bag you want and then make the money fit. You'll be happier for it later.

Sleeping bag brands. There are a zillion manufacturers to choose from. Here are a few good ones (addresses in the Sources Appendix).

Gerry, as in tents. Same qualities and qualifications.

North Face builds mostly mummies, and fine quality, too.

Sierra Design makes mountaineers' gear with high-class options. They peddle high-rent personal furniture that works extremely well and makes you look like Stewart Granger.

Holubar is a specialty outfit catering to hard-core explorers and backwoods types. Their gear is made by elves who commit hara-kiri if they drop a stitch. Best-built bags on the market.

Alpine Designs builds a versatile line of sleeping bags for the summer soldier, with many good features for the nomad. Some of their designs approach perfection for biker's use.

Antarctic Imports builds bags for the people who talk to penguins at the South Pole. They're located in New Zealand and you can save a bundle by buying from them — even with import duty. Their bags have some idiosyncrasies, like short zippers and strange shapes, but the nomads I know who use them would kill for them.

Black's makes bags with the same scrupulous care they use on their tents. They are also among the least expensive manufacturers of good bags. Dollar for dollar, it's hard to beat them.

Frostline offers a do-it-yourself line that includes sleeping bags. If you have basic sewing skills, you can make a superior bag for less money than you can buy an inferior one. I know of a two-wheeler who uses Frostline's bag, tent, and down-filled jacket, for which he paid about what a jacket alone would have cost store-boughten.

Ocate is another do-it-yourself manufacturer, but they specialize in a strange-looking bag made of polyurethane. The thing is hell to roll up, and a little on the heavy side, but it works fantastically well and costs about half of what a down-filled bag would. And with polyurethane, you don't need an air mattress, which brings up another point.

Jesse James on Sleep and Shelter

One of the few authenticated "facts" about Ol' Jess, as he was known to some folks, was that he hated to be woke up before he was finished sleeping. He once had a conversation with his brother Frank about the relative merits of brush and buffalo chips as bedding material. The conclusion was that neither was worth a damn.

That situation still holds true for the person who sleeps close to the ground. The persistent dream of a soft bed of pine nedles is mostly just that — a dream. Pine needles are seasonal, regional, and overrated. Most often, the nomad beds down on surfaces ranging from lumpy ground with stubble on it to gravel and shale. I once rode into Picacho Peak in the Lincoln National Forest in Arizona and duly went over to the "Tenters Only" area. The ground there, friend, was *flint*. Not chunk flint, but arrowhead flint. And that's a common condition in most of this country's organized state and national parks.

What do you put under your bag? The two options are air mattress and foam pads.

Air mattresses were most likely invented by someone with a warped mind. They are hard to inflate, do not insulate at all, and all of them go flat at 2:30 in the morning. I have tried everything from the 98¢ beach-float things to self-inflating rigs that cost $13, and none of them work right.

The only value of an air mattress is that it deflates and stores easily. And when it stays up, an air mattress is almost comfortable.

Foam pads are comfortable, your bag won't slip off them, and they insulate well. But they are heavy and do not compress at all. To be effective, a foam pad has to be at least a couple of inches thick, 18 inches wide, and 3½ feet long. When you roll that up in the morning to load it on your mount, you have a bundle a foot and a half wide and a foot and a half in diameter.

The best solution I've seen so far is a stuff called Insulite. It's a foamlike material with about six times the insulation value of rubber or polyurethane foam, and it will keep the cold, cold ground at a distance. But it will also let you feel every pebble under you. Its value lies in the fact that you can use much thinner sheets than with foam, making it feasible to roll and pack. A ⅜-inch thick piece of Insulite will keep you warm at the contact points in weather down to 20 degrees. It's expensive, though. An 18″ × 42″ × ⅜″ pad will cost you nearly $10.

But don't scrimp on any of your sleeping gear, especially the part between you and the rocks. I have tested Jesse James's conclusion about brush and buffalo chips and he's right; it not only isn't worth a damn but it leaves you with an interesting aroma for about a week.

Augutendarssak and the Six-Day Blizzard

Eventually, you will find yourself trapped by cold, rough weather for a few days. It simply isn't practical to spend that much time in your sleeping bag. How do you keep warm?

In Greenland, up above Cape Atholl, a friend of mine got caught out on the ice by a blizzard that lasted six days. He coped by killing a bear, slitting it open, and crawling inside for the duration. This method has the same drawback as staying in your sleeping bag — lack of mobility. Plus the added problem of locating a convenient bear. The heat involved was Augutendarssak's own, with the bear acting as insulation. In his home, he added another heat source, and that's what you must do. The source you use is a catalytic heater. These gadgets produce flameless, nontoxic heat through chemical action. The importance of those two characteristics can't be overemphasized, because any other form of heating plant is an invitation to your own funeral. The camping manuals never tell you about the long spells of cold you will encounter, and few beginning nomads think about the subject. Consequently, when the cold spell arrives, there is nothing around designed to deal with it. The usual response is to crank up your cooking stove or to build a fire in the skillet.

This approach results in better than 85 percent of all camping fatalities.

Fires consume oxygen and produce toxic gases. A wet tent is a sealed tent. A sealed tent with an open fire in it is a closed, oxygen-consuming system. And if the fire gets the oxygen, you don't. Tents, and most of the things in them, are very, very flammable. I once saw a family-sized tent burn to the ground before I could sprint the 20 yards to it. That's something under six seconds.

Catalytic heaters are heavy and bulky, use expensive fuel, and are of limited use unless you are doing the Yukon. But if you even think you might get yourself into a position where you would be tempted to light a fire in your house, buy a heater instead.

What They Didn't Tell You About Valley Forge

If all this seems to emphasize the drastic aspects of two-wheel nomadics, remember that you are preparing for the worst times, and that these times will normally be few and far between. The purpose of preparation is to make them bearable when they come, just as you own a raincoat even though it doesn't rain every day — unless you live in New Orleans.

Keep in mind also the prevalence of myth. Most "hard times" get harder in the telling than they were in the living. We have a great piece of folklore that tells us that George Washington's troops were starving and frozen that winter in Valley Forge, and that many men deserted because of this. But in reality, most of the deserters left because their hitch was up, because their farms and families were nearby, and because not many of them believed in Washington's cause in the first place. Contemporary accounts by men who served that winter tell of hardships and short rations, but nothing like the myth that's come down to us.

Generally speaking, most experienced nomads avoid heat in their homes, relying on personal acclimatization and enjoying the weather. If you are faced with a question of survival, as opposed to comfort, you can heat your house thusly: Build a fire outside. Heat up a large pot or skillet full of stones. Bring this inside and place it in the center of the tent on something nonflammable. You have a dry heat source, flameless and nontoxic, that will be effective for up to an hour. If you have two pots, keep one inside and one on the fire, changing them as the one inside cools.

The complete motorcycle nomad, then, will have a tent or shelter that suits his personal needs and the climate he will encounter. It will be the best he can afford. He will have a bag or bags of the design best suited to his sleeping habits, and something to put between the bag and the tent floor or ground. He will have a catalytic heater if he expects to be tent-bound for any length of time and will under no circumstances consider an open fire inside his house.

Information: Sources Appendix, other riders, manufacturers.

7. FOOD

The Hard-Core Cooker

You can tell the true nomad by his proficiency at camp cooking. A real hard-core outdoor freak can build a wood fire from scratch and whip up a gourmet meal on it in less time than a weekend camper can get his Coleman three-burner assembled and cranked up. I have seen everything from a trout amandine dinner for four with all the trimmings to a six-course supper topped with Baked Alaska prepared by experienced nomads with nothing more complicated than a skillet and a couple of pots. Granted, it takes practice, much patience, and a flair for gustatory creation, but the point is that it can be done. The camping manuals are full of "46 ways to cook beans in a pot" meals, and this is fine as far as it goes. But the nomad will get just as tired of beans as his sedentary brethren, and it is good to remember that you can cook damn near anything in camp that you could in an apartment. The limits are your own skill as a chef and the versatility of your tools.

How to Determine Your Kitchen Needs

Cooking is the process of applying heat to food. Most camp cooking employs the two basic methods of frying or boiling. For many people, however, an unvaried diet of boiled and fried foods will grow old with some rapidity. Eventually, there will be a craving for baked goods, a roast, poached eggs, and such. This craving will drive you either up the wall or into a restaurant.

Your kitchen needs, then, are determined by your diet.

Sit down and make an accurate list of what sorts of food you have eaten regularly in the last year and of how they are prepared. Figure what percentage of your diet consists of fresh or uncooked foods, what percentage of fried, or broiled, of baked, etc. If any form of prepared food occupies less than 10 percent of your diet, disregard it; you'll eat that in restaurants. Of the remainder, how much can be done in one type of tool? (For example, you can stew, boil and pot-roast in one heavy pot with a lid.) When you are done with this, you will have a list of cooking vessels you will need.

Now figure what your average meal consists of. Do you like steak and potatoes with a side vegetable and rolls? Or perhaps fried fish with broccoli and a cup of tea? Is your breakfast a toast-and-coffee affair, or do you like juice, bacon, eggs, and the works? This list will tell you how many of each type of cooking vessel you need. I, for instance, like a southern breakfast of eggs, sausage, grits, biscuits and coffee, with perhaps a glass of juice. I can do the sausage and the eggs in one pan, but I need separate vessels for the grits and the coffee.

The object is to figure out the maximum number of vessels of each type you need, then throw away anything ridiculous. If you really need four saucepans, you'll find a way to get along on two!

Next, figure your accessory tools. That means carving knives, stew ladles, can openers, two-prong forks and suchlike. Then figure out what you need for eating utensils — plates, knives and forks, spoons, cups and glasses. Finally, remember the auxiliary tools like salt and pepper shakers, water carriers, and storage containers. More on food storage in a moment.

What to Cook On and In

Once you have a fair idea of the types and numbers of kitchen tools you require, you must give thought to how you can best fill those requirements within the motorcycle nomad's frame of limitations and to the second aspect of food preparation, the heat source.

First, the tools: The two approaches are cooking sets and random pieces. Depending on how specialized your diet is, you may find one approach better than the other. Generally, the broader the cooking spectrum your diet has, the better a cooking set will serve you.

Cooking sets are vessels designed for the traveler. They are made of lightweight metals like aluminum, are usually designed so that they will nest and store as a unit, and have things like folding handles and locking tops. Many come with eating weapons included, which solves one of your problems for you. They can be purchased in a variety of combinations of vessels but most contain a plate, a cup, a skillet, and a pot with lid. Cooking sets come in one-person, two-person, four-person, and whole-gang sizes. The larger the size, the greater the variety of vessels. The rule on cooking sets is: get a size larger than the number of people you expect to feed regularly. If you will be traveling alone, get a two-person kit; if you are taking a friend, get a four-person kit, etc. The added versatility will make you happy when you get that urge to blow it all with a five-course feed, and if you are on the road for very long, you'll have the urge to cook for the friends around your fire some night.

The advantages of cooking sets are their light weight and proper design, their ease of storage, and their versatility. The disadvantages are that they are expensive, that they are a little fragile — once dented, they won't nest properly, and that their light gauge makes cooking an interesting event at times.

To amplify this last point: cooking fires in the open are less controllable than home ranges. Temperature definition is not as fine. With a thin aluminum skillet, a heat flare-up will turn your nice morning bacon into charcoal before you can catch it. (The good side of this same problem is that you can heat large masses like stew and water much more rapidly.)

Random piecing gives you more options in the composition of your cooking tools. You can carry a heavy iron skillet, a light-gauge pot and a heavy one, maybe a Teflon griddle for your pancakes. This system also gives you a chance to save some money, since you can often scrounge what you need or find it less expensively than in a matched nesting cooking set.

The disadvantages are obvious: bulk, difficulty of storage, weight, etc.

On the whole, if you are an experienced cook who enjoys the sensual aspects of food, build your own set. If you are new to camp cooking or regard food as a necessity rather than an art form, get a cooking set.

Heat Sources

This is another place where the myths get in the way. I don't think I've ever seen a camping book, a scout manual, or a park directory that didn't show the Happy Camper broiling something — probably his fingers — over a neatly laid out wood fire. In these pictures, the smoke is either nonexistent or it rises obediently straight up into the cloudless sky.

The hard facts are that (a) open-fire cookery is an art

No cooking in your tent!

that takes a long time to master, (b) the majority of state and national campgrounds either won't allow it or will only allow it if you supply your own wood, (c) usable fuel is difficult or impossible to find in the wilds unless you know what you are doing, (d) the ecological dangers of forest fires and land-stripping are way out of proportion to the meal you'll gain, and (e) those skies are not always cloudless.

Open wood fires have their place for the two-wheel nomad, but it is a limited place. Given the opportunity, I will always cook over wood, simply because of the esthetic values and the good vibes. But you cannot and should not depend on available-fuel fires for your day-to-day living. I don't and probably wouldn't if I could for fear of becoming one of those people I can't stand — the ones who clomp through the land as if it were an amusement put there for their personal use.

There are two heat-source systems you can use: camp stoves and charcoal.

Camp stoves run on bottled gas and come in all sorts of configurations. You can get little one-bottle numbers made for mountaineers that fold up into teeny-weeny lumps, two-burner, three-burner, and even four-burner models. You can get them with or without housings, with or without grills, with or without accessories, and so forth into redundancy.

The advantages of camp stoves are their controlled flame, which gives you fine tuning in your cookery, their all-weather versatility, their ease of operation and cleaning, and their universality. You can get parts, service, and fuel for most makes of camp stove anywhere in the world.

Their prime disadvantage is that even the skeleton models are heavy and cannot be compressed smaller than the fuel bottle itself. The really compact kind — those made for backpackers and such folk — are often fragile and difficult to use because the stewpot falls off when you stir in the chopped lizard. The big, stable models have to be moved around with a crane.

There are happy mediums, though. Some camp-stove manufacturers build models with heavy wire frames instead of sheet metal ones, and a few make them with configurations that allow the gas bottle(s) to store inside and then brace outside while in use.

Most nomads who use camp stoves — and that's most nomads — use a wire-frame, two-burner unit. Propane fuel is preferable to white gas because it is more available and a little cheaper.

The other alternative in heat sources is dangerous, clumsy, more expensive, less controllable and efficient, and the one I use. It is charcoal.

Charcoal costs more than bottled gas, BTU for BTU. It is very bulky to carry around, slow to use, and gets your hands dirty. It is dangerous because you have to carry around a can of starter, which is not the best stuff to have sloshing over your hot exhaust pipes when a truck runs over you.

I have no logical reason for using it. I just started doing so one day when I ran out of bottled gas in Hondo, Texas, and haven't changed back. The only value I can see in the stuff is that it is a little homier out on the range than a portable Bunsen burner. It's a more comfortable thing to stare into at night. I would not recommend it to anyone unless he were suffering from terminal romance, but it *is* an alternative and I so record it here.

Camp stoves cost $4 to $35.

Good brands are Sears, Coleman, Lumnigaz.

What to Cook: How the Romans Conquered the World

The Romans excelled at nothing. They are noted for their prowess as logicians, yet the Goths were better; they were superb fighting men, yet they lost more battles than they won; they were fantastically well-armed for their day, yet most of their opponents had as good.

But the Romans were practical men, and that trait brought most of the known world under Roman rule. One aspect of Roman practicality was the respect they gave to food and its handling. They allowed men to farm instead of soldier when the season warranted it. They scheduled their campaigns to avoid manpower conflicts during harvests. When they took a region, they secured the granaries and food stores first. The first directive of

Roman quartermastering was to carry the foodstuffs that weren't locally available and take the rest from the inhabitants.

This principle applies equally to the motorcycle nomad. The backpacker has to carry the grocery store with him. You don't. You need carry only those things that you aren't sure of getting along the road, spices, and such things as can't be bought in one- or two-day quantities. For example, oatmeal seldom comes in two-serving packages. Nor salt, nor eggs, nor potatoes.

But many things do, and many others come in compacted form. When assessing your diet, look at the foods in your daily menu and divide them into items that can be purchased day-to-day and items that you must carry. Note also which of them can be bought dehydrated or compacted. Most of this kind of chow suffers in the taste department but offers the same nutritional value as whole foods.

You will find that if you avoid shopping in large chain stores you can buy food in small quantities with little hassle. You can get eggs by the half-dozen in small stores, potatoes and onions and such by the unit, fruit by the unit, etc. The trick is to find a friendly store and look poor.

When you have figured out what foods you will have to store and carry, work out the space needed to do so. Get a rough "cubic" volume and translate this into component areas (how much for rice, how much for powdered milk, etc.) Bear in mind that a loaf of bread is slightly flexible but still takes up a large piece of space, but you can wrap rolls individually and stick them anywhere. I used to put two on top of the engine housing in the morning and they would be warm and slow-baked in time for lunch.

The general rule on what to cook is: avoid things that require refrigeration, things that can be bought only in bulk, and things that require special tools to prepare. (Poached eggs take an egg poacher.)

Pitfalls of Outdoor Cooking

Remember, eventually you'll have to do it in the rain and mud.

Outdoor cooks either go along with the weather or shut it out. That is, you develop a kitchen style that will work in any weather or you develop a sheltered kitchen. The former is less reliable, but the latter takes extra gear.

If you want to rough it, I'd advise you to take along a heavy pot with a tight lid. This will allow you to use the "Dutch oven" recipes. Dutch-oven cooking involves digging a pit, filling it with fire, sticking your pot of food in, and shoveling dirt over the whole mess for a few hours. The advantage of this system is that your fire is underground and will burn nicely through all but torrential downpours. This is an old and honored nomads' cooking method and has lasted for good reason. Pit-cooked stews and beans have a certain flavor you can't get with any other method, and that gets important on the road.

If you prefer to shut the weather out, you need a shelter for your kitchen. This means a small tarp, since you do *not* cook in your tent. The tarp should be less than 3 feet on a side, preferably 2 feet (for weight and space savings) and should be thoroughly fireproof. Don't bother about waterproofing it as the heat from beneath will keep it dry. Remember that your object is to keep the rain off the rutabagas, not you.

If you have assembled your kitchen by the random-piecing method and have included a heavy pot or skillet in your selection, consider taking that small tarp anyway. The variety it will give you, weatherwise, will be worth the penalties in tonnage.

There are any number of good books around on the

subject of camp cooking. Most are useless for the two-wheel nomad as far as their recommendations on gear go, but all will acquaint you with the wonderful variety of mistakes you can make when learning the art of outdoor cookery. Truck on down to the library and read four. Anything that any three of them tell you, you can believe. Concentrate on recurrent themes instead of the clever little tricks; you'll develop your own tricks as you go along, and they'll seem as absurd to someone else as the ones in the books do to you.

What Folds, Weighs Six Ounces, and Bakes?

There are two final gadgets to consider, and one complete approach to road kitchens. The first of the gadgets is a camp oven.

Camp ovens are aluminum reflectors that fold and bend in various ways to trap reflected heat from your fire. They are light and small but somewhat delicate and must be stored with care. However, if your diet includes the delightful world of baked goods, you might seriously consider taking a camp oven with you. I usually carry one, even though I use it only about once a month. There is a certain snob appeal in being able to bake a chocolate cake in the middle of nowhere, using what looks like a collection of TV dinner trays with hinges.

The only real problem with reflector ovens is that they are designed for use with open fires. A gas unit doesn't put out enough radiant heat to make a reflector work.

There are a couple of "ovens" designed to be used with gas burners, but I've found that their prime value is in the production of chocolate-flavored charcoal.

The second gadget I'd advocate is a grill of some sort. Few campsites have conveniently placed flat rocks to put your skillet on, and you sometimes want an open fire even if you have a gas burner. I made a grill out of half of a refrigerator tray and it has worked perfectly for two years. It mounts on the bottom of the luggage rack, out of the way, and has proven its usefulness many times.

Mio Kimura's Method

I once traveled with a Japanese lady named Mio, whose diet consisted of much fish, fruit, and rice, and was one of the most flavorful and healthful I have ever eaten. Her kitchen consisted of a single pot, a knife, a bowl, and some chopsticks. She could take these tools, a handful of food, and about enough heat to warm your hands over, and produce absolute symphonies of taste and nutrition. And in about a third the time it took me to set up my stove. She could — and did — put her whole kitchen in a large handbag, food and all.

If you are not partial to oriental cooking, or do not want to learn this simple and delightful method of preparing your meals, you might still bear in mind that there are easy ways to feed yourself without large investments in equipment. What I have described is the "complete" nomad's kitchen, and you can get along nicely with less.

More information can be found in the Sources Appendix.

Wisdom

"*You are what you eat.*"

"*A well-fed man is a happy man.*"

"*Look to your stomach and your life will tend itself.*"

8.

LIGHTS

Man is the only animal that consistently stays up past his bedtime. He has never really decided whether he is a nocturnal being or a creature of the sunlight. Consequently, he has spent most of history trying to be both. This has led to the invention of sleeping pills, law courts, wake-up pills, bars, and artificial illumination.

We have not yet even faintly approached a "natural" illumination source on a commercial basis. The wattage needed to give an equivalent of sunlight to even a small room is fantastic. The expense of lighting a home to nature's standards would be prohibitive for all but Greek shipping magnates. We think inferior night-lighting is good, when all we have demonstrated is the tolerance of our own eyes. This is one reason why 65 percent of us wear eyeglasses before we are thirty.

Two-wheel nomadics makes exceptional demands on your vision. When you ride, your eyes are subject to either the effects of wind and dust or of peering through layers of glass or plastic. If, for example, you wear prescription glasses, goggles over them, and a windshield on your mount, you are trying to see through three separate devices that cut the available light as much as 15 percent each. You seldom notice the effect of this reduction in light directly, but by the end of a day's ride your eyes will let you know their displeasure.

Then, in camp at night, you read yourself to sleep by candlelight.

Lighting is not a subject you give much thought to when preparing for the road. A flashlight is about as far as most folks go. But then, we seldom envision ourselves with insomnia, or with a tent full of friends in an all-night rap session, or with an extended emergency. But these things occur, and they occur to almost every nomad. A friendly — and usable — light can make them easier to deal with.

How Much, How Long, How Often?

Determining your lighting needs brings up another three-vector system. How much light do you need for a given task, how long will you be on the road, and how often will you need a lot of light? These factors intertwine, and at their intersection you will find your ideal light source.

How much? Do you write a lot of postcards in the evening? Or read yourself to sleep? Or knit? Or make Chinese puzzles? Do you, in fact, do anything close or precise with your hands or anything extended (like reading) with your eyes on a regular basis? If so, you will require a high-illumination light source. True, you *can* do almost anything by candlelight; but I don't know of a single state that will issue a motorcycle driver's license to a blind person.

If you do anything precise or close, but only sporadically — which means less than once a week — you can get away with a medium-illumination light source. Your eyes can recover from a two-hour perusal of *The Sensuous Motorcycle* if they are only asked to do so occasionally.

If you do nothing whatsoever that would strain your eyes, you can get by with low-illumination light sources.

Consider this, however, only if you sleep like the proverbial poled ox, are not accident prone, and are half wombat.

How long? The time factor enters into your determinations because the potential of encountering an emergency or a personal need for strong illumination goes up exponentially as the length of your voyage increases. If you are on the road for a week, you are not likely to have to perform an appendectomy on yourself by candlelight; a summer-long journey increases the odds in favor of surgery.

Incidentally, poor light is the cause of a lot of nocturnal accidents. I once came near to slicing my arm off at the elbow for want of sufficient light. I had only a flashlight to work with, and I leave it to your imagination to picture how much fun it can be trying to stitch up a cut one-handed with a bloody flashlight in your teeth.

How often? Again, the more close work you do and the longer you travel, the greater will be your frequency of need for good lighting. As you approach full-time nomadic living, your lighting needs will become as critical as they do in a house. This is simply because you will be performing the full range of living functions, from washing clothes to repairing the furniture. After a time, you will chafe under bad lighting to the point where you will cut corners and make mistakes, and this is a dangerous proposition.

Vector your habits against your proposed travel time and against the frequency of your high-illumination needs. If you need strong light infrequently or for nonemergencies (letter writing, etc.), you may well get by without high-light sources. Most campgrounds, for instance, have toilets or laundry facilities that are lit at night. You can do postcards, clothes patching and that sort of thing quite well in the john. If you plan to spend most of your time in the boondocks, though, get a good light.

High Light, Medium Light, Low Light

How do you classify light sources? Roughly, in descending order of illuminative power, you have electrics, gas, and open flame. However, this is not always accurate. A two-burner gas mantle lantern will put out a lot more light than a battery-powered electric. And there are even high-light candles.

In general, it runs like this:

High light	Two-burner gas mantle lamps. Plug-in electric lights. Four/five–battery flashlights.
Medium Light	Single-burner gas mantle lamps. One/three–battery flashlights. Four-unit candle lamps.
Low light	Small battery lamps. Candle lamps. Kerosene or oil lamps.

The Inevitable Coleman

Every camper who chooses something stronger than a flashlight opts for a gas mantle lamp. There are good reasons for this. Coleman-type lamps offer an awful lot of light, are relatively cheaply fueled, and are portable. A big two-mantle job will turn even the blackest woods into a stage set for 100 yards around. And there are times when that's a desirable quality. Even a single-mantle lamp will provide more light than most battery-powered sources or any combination of candles.

But for the biker they present quite a variety of problems. They are large and bulky, thus hard to pack, and are clumsy in the bargain. They all have glass housings, which will invariably break and render the lamp useless. They take at least 30 seconds to fire up, and most of them take nearer a full minute: not the best condition when you suspect that the noise outside your tent is a bear. The fuel for gas lamps comes in cans, which must either be toted around with you — and they are almost explosively flammable — or thrown away with one lamp filling used, which gets expensive. When improperly started, most of them will produce open flame and clouds of oily smoke to grease the inside of your domicile with soot — not to mention the golden opportunities they present for cremation.

Still, a gas mantle lantern is the highest light source that is portable in the woods.

The final problem with gas lamps is that they hiss and stink. Hiss loudly and obnoxiously and stink enough to flavor your clothes and rations.

Gas mantle lamps cost $11 to $34. Good brands: Coleman (best), Lumnigaz, Dietz.

Candles

Candles have many advantages as a nomadic light source. They are inexpensive, available everywhere, are esthetically pleasing, and don't take up much room. All they fail to do well is produce light.

Open candles are a danger. What you use are candle lanterns. These are constructions of metal and wire with isinglass light panels and are designed to hold a candle in windproof splendor. They were originally built for backpackers and mountaineers, and many models fold or compress into spaces little larger than the candle itself. You can get them in one-, two-, and four-candle sizes, but the best are the single-wick numbers. The reason is simply that four single-candle lanterns can be stored in four places, as opposed to having to shove one large, bulky lantern into your duffle. Also, you can hang four lanterns in four spots for the best distribution of light.

A single-candle lantern is sufficient light for dressing by, for groping through your packs, for making love by, for eating by, and for close work that takes less than ten minutes.

Two candles allow you to write short letters, trim your beard, give a massage, and like that.

Three candles are good for long letters, one chapter in a novel, looking up something in this book, and throwing the I Ching.

Four candles are the insomnia special, used for long stares into the side of the tent, delivering babies, writing your will, solving the world's problems, and planning in great detail just how you're going to get that trout tomorrow morning.

If you go with candle lanterns, by all means get the folding models, and get the ones that take those big, cheap white candles you can get in the grocery store. Many mountaineer's lanterns are designed for the little votive-type candles, which produce an echo of light but no real illumination.

Candle lanterns cost $4.50 to $9. Good brands: many.

Electrics, Pro and Con

The best light available is electric, also the worst. Plug-in light is the highest concentrate of illumination the society has yet produced for commercial use. Battery electrics are a bastard compromise.

Battery light comes in the "flashlight" and the "lantern" configurations. The former produces high illumination over a narrow beam with some range. The latter produces general or flood illumination over a large sphere for limited range. Flashlights are good and useful tools; lanterns are useless.

To illuminate a sphere with any degree of potency requires a lot of power. In batteries, this spells weight and cost. Battery-powered lanterns run off a single, huge battery or off a series of smaller batteries. Either way the cost is large and the life expectancy small. Most of these units are expensive to buy, running from $10 to $30, expensive to fuel, as the batteries cost up to $5 per replacement, and wear out rapidly. The better ones give light for 20 hours for about $3.50. A Coleman gas mantle lamp will give twice the light for the same period for about 35¢.

There is no light source as heavy and bulky as a battery lantern.

With most of the things I discuss in this book, I give a pro and con side. There is no pro side to battery lanterns as far as I'm concerned.

Flashlights, however, are another story. A good flashlight will provide as strong a cone of illumination as you need for most jobs, will do it fairly cheaply, and will be infinitely useful in more ways than you would imagine.

A "good" flashlight is a three- or four-battery number with a metal reflector — not coated plastic. It will be sturdy, preferably unbreakable, will have a ring to hang it by, and will have a strong switch that resists accidental on/off status changes.

As a source of general light, flashlights are next to useless. But for directional light, they can't be beat.

Avoid the temptation to buy cheapies or small, two-battery flashlights. Avoid the big, fancy ones that have blinkers and whistle "Hail to the Chief." This is a functional, important tool, and yours should be chosen for usability, not looks.

Finally, let's take a look at plug-in electrics.

Sneaky gadgets. The prime drawback of plug-in lighting is that you have to have a place to plug it into. Believe it or not, that's not as big a problem as you'd imagine.

Most nomads, whatever their intentions when they set out, wind up spending one night out of five in a formal campground. Almost all these places have electric connections of one sort or another. And for these times, you carry that fine old nomad's tool, a light bulb!

Actually, the rig consists of (a) a bulb, (b) a socket, and (c) some cord. The bulb can be anything you desire, but it should be sufficiently strong to allow you to do *any* work you anticipate doing. The socket can be anything made for the purpose also, but the best ones are those drop-proof mechanics' sockets (to keep the bulb safe when packed away). The cord on those mechanics' lights is usually a heavy, industrial one. This is fine but it is also clumsy and bulky.

My light bulb plug-in system consists of a 100-watt soft-light bulb in a small tin can with a hook on the top. It is connected to a light-gauge cord that runs to the tent wall and plugs in there. In the tent wall itself, I have sewn an industrial plug-in that takes cords from both sides. For outside, I have a *sheathed*, medium-gauge line 25 feet long, with a grounded plug on the jack end. The tent aperture has been coated liberally with a rubber-based sealer for insulation against both shock and water leakage, and the jack end of the outside cord has a sheath made from a surgical glove.

My entire lighting system consists of this plug-in affair, a four-battery, rubber-sheathed, indestructable flashlight, and three candle lanterns. The candles take care of general illumination out in the swamps, the flashlight takes care of general portable light needs and also provides emergency high-intensity light, and the plug-in gives me all the comforts of home when I'm in a campground. All together, this light system takes up less space and weight than a Coleman lamp and its fuel, and it can be stored in odd cracks and pockets. By this combination of lights, I have delivered babies, done drawings, and written some of this book.

Plug-in lights cost (roughly) $4.75.

Wisdom

No animal has night and day sight both.

All nomadic societies cast the blind out to die.

Candles cost less than eye transplants.

9.
TOOLS and sundry

The nomad carries his tools with him, for he faces certain tasks that his urban brother doesn't — such as breaking down and setting up his house. He must also be his own repairman more often than not, since breakages tend to occur in out-of-the-way places.

Tools fall into two categories, bike and house. Bike tools are meant for repair and maintenance, and house tools for the day-to-day peculiarities of nomadic existence.

We'll take the bike tools first.

Finite Bike Tools

To be absolutely sure of being able to repair your mount under any conditions, you would have to tow a trailer containing a complete workshop and another bike. This presents obvious difficulties. What you do instead is carry a number of basic tools and enough spare parts to cover the most likely emergencies. You also carry certain analytic devices to allow you to assess the trouble that comes to visit you. The trick is to be prepared enough to get yourself down the road to professional help, however spastically, and to do this in such a manner that you aren't towing that trailer full of parts and gadgets. Tools being heavy items and hard to store, that isn't as simple a trick as it first appears. Here's how you go about performing it.

Basics

Motorcycles are assemblies of parts attached either permanently or temporarily. Permanent attachments are welded, temporary ones either bolted or screwed. An engine, for example, can be disassembled because it is bolted together; a frame cannot because it is welded. On the road, you will be able to cope only with disassemblable parts. Therefore, your tools will be designed primarily for bolting and unbolting things. Screwdrivers, impact wrenches, wrench sets, pliers, ratchet drivers — all are built to make bolting and unbolting easier. Your first set of basic tools, then, are your bolters.

Second come maintenance tools. They are designed to keep your mount in good health. They include adjustment devices, balms and unguents (like plastic polish for your windshield), and feeding tools. (Some bikes have awkward filler caps for oil and require a funnel.)

Finally, you need tools for analysis. This is almost always an electrical consideration. Mechanical problems tend to manifest themselves simply and in plain language, but electrics work in mysterious ways guaranteed either to teach you patience or drive you to hitchhiking.

You have, then, bolters, maintenance tools, and tools for analysis and diagnosis.

Nuts and Bolts

Your first, heaviest, and most expensive tool is an impact driver. This is a barrel-shaped thing with a striking surface on one end and a holder on the other. You insert a screwdriver head in the holder, twist the barrel in the direction you wish the tool to rotate, and hit the other end with a hammer. The tool converts this linear motion into rotary motion and — hopefully — turns the object screw without stripping the head, which is what impact drivers are all about. Most impact drivers come with an assortment of regular-blade and Phillips-head screwdrivers. They cost from $8 to $14, weight a couple of pounds, and do the job right. This is the absolute basic tool. Get one if you carry nothing else. Consider that if you have an internal problem and have to get into the engine cases, for instance, you will be helpless if you strip the heads on the casing bolts. A lot of bike builders, particularly the Japanese, save money by using bolts and screws made of pressed cardboard or somesuch, and they peel off like butter when attacked with an ordinary screwdriver. So the

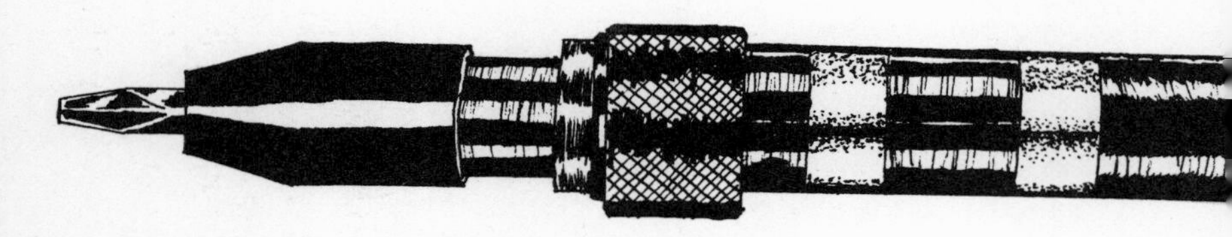

An impact driver.

moral is spend the bread, get an impact driver.

You will also need two regular screwdrivers, a long-shank, thin-blade model and a short-shank, heavy-blade model. The long one is for getting into those impossible places, and the shorty is for getting into those other impossible places — the ones where you need a third hand and a prehensile tail. Buy the best you can afford and try for insulated rubber handles.

You need two pairs of pliers, a needle-nose and a blunt-nose. The needle-nose pair is for electrical work and for minor surgery, and the blunt-nose is for those places you can't get into with your vise grips. Both pairs should have a wire-cutting arrangement, and the needle-nose should have a wire stripper built in.

Vise grips are adjustable pliers that clamp and hold in a locked position. This is the second most useful tool you will own because it has literally hundreds of emergency uses — some of which will be detailed in Chapter Fifteen. Get a good pair and treat them with respect.

Finally, you need a set of sockets and a ratchet driver. A ratchet driver is a lever that holds in one direction of rotation and gives in the other, with a switch for changing the direction of hold. It fits over a socket, which fits over

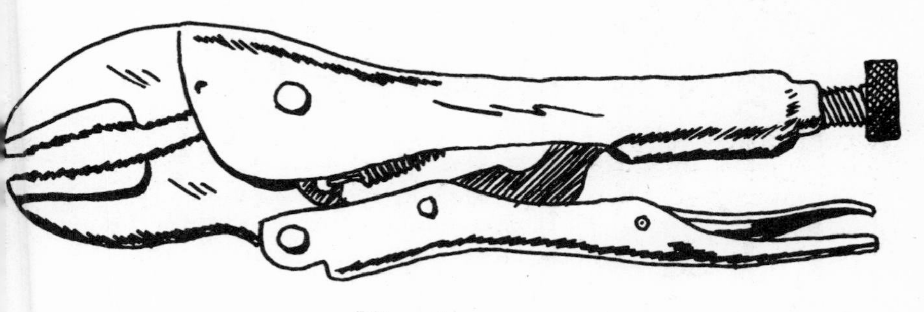

Vise grips.

the bolt you're trying to get off or on, and gives you those Charles Atlas muscles necessary for the job.

When buying your sockets, be sure to check your mount for the types of heads the bolts have. Bolts come in inch measurements in America, metrics in Europe and Asia, and a bastard size called Whitworth in Britain. Someday, when the world gets saner, everything will be in metrics, but for now, check your bike out.

Check also for the *sizes* of your bolts. Most newer bikes have standardized construction and come in about four bolt-head sizes, but some don't, particularly the antiquated and English machines. If you buy your sockets in a set, chances are that you will be missing that 13 mm that you need to take the seat mounts loose or the ⅜-inch without which you cannot remove the pretzel-bent handlebars.

Check the axle nuts! Many are in a size for which you can buy a socket. Same goes for your sparkplugs. If you can't get the wheel off, a simple flat tire will cripple you, as will a fouled plug.

Do not carry a set of open- or box-end wrenches because they are redundant. The places you cannot reach with your socket set will be reachable with patience and your vise grips. Remember the weight and space penalties.

Now, maintenance tools.

Upkeep

Speaking of getting that wheel off, your first maintenance tool is a set of tire irons. These are little metal blades that slip under the rim of your tire and separate it from the wheel. They cost a buck or so apiece and none of them work without much cursing and sweating, but they are better than a couple of screwdrivers because they won't puncture your only spare inner tube in the middle of Akela Flats, Arizona. A better alternative is a super tire iron, which is a kind of tire-changing crowbar with odd-shaped ends. One end takes the tire off, the other puts it on. The super tire iron is too big and heavy to store anywhere decent, but it works 100 percent and I wouldn't be without one. They cost about $3 and are available at most bike shops. (Incidentally, I keep mine taped across my handlebars. It's out of the way and tends to discourage the odd biker-baiter.)

Next, you need feeding tools, which means that funnel I mentioned — if your mount requires one — chain lube, polishes and such, and whatever oiling devices fit you and your mount best.

Hint: An ex-Yamaha-racing-team man once told me that the company tested every chain lubricant from commercial mixes to butter and found that plain Vaseline works best. Nice, since Vaseline costs less per pound than the commercial squirters do per ounce.

Last in your maintenance tools section are adjustment devices, by which I mean whatever special tools are required for keeping your particular mount in tune. This includes plug gappers, valve-clearance guides for four-bangers, chain breakers, timing pins, etc.

You will find that the tool kits that come with new bikes have low-grade tools, but the right ones. Most will include special tools necessary for the operation of your make mount—like axle-nut removal systems. If your socket set and vise grips can't handle the specific job of a given exotic tool, keep the tool. If they can, throw the tool away or leave it home.

The exceptions to this are English bikes with Whitworth tools, which are expensive to buy and hard to locate; Moto-Guzzi and BMWs, whose tools are of superior quality; Czech or Russian bikes, which have a lot of weird tools.

And last, diagnostic tools.

Electrics

Beside your insulated needle-nose pliers and insulated screwdrivers, you will need a testlamp. It consists of two insulated wires connected to a miniwattage bulb (6 or 12 volt, to match your bike's electrical system) on one end and alligator clips on the other. It costs about 45¢ to make, and its usage is covered in Chapter Fifteen. You will also need a roll of electrical tape and a small roll of insulated wire in a gauge roughly compatible with your mount's own nerve system. There are many, many tools needed for complete electrical troubleshooting, but you

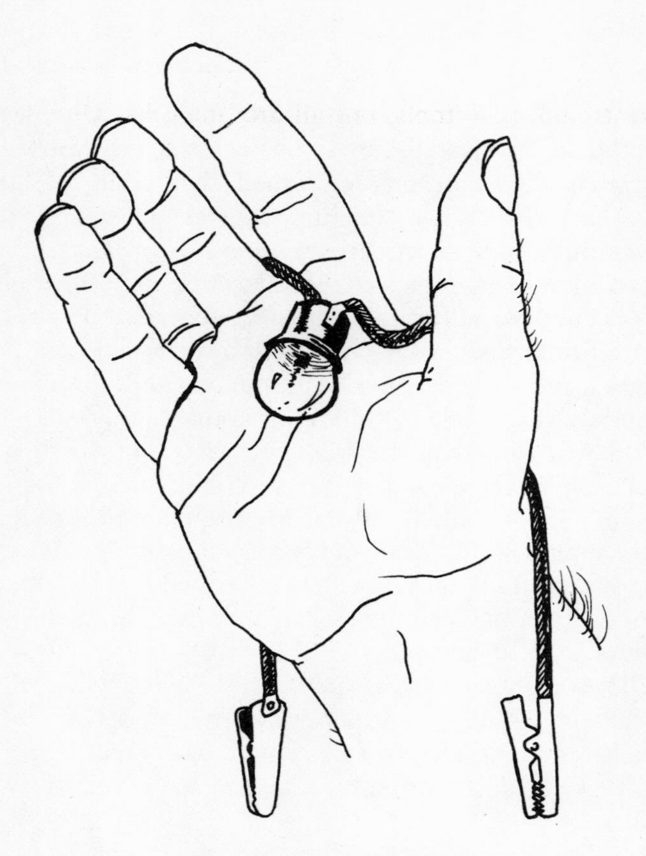

A circuit test gadget.

haven't the room to carry them. What you must do, then, is develop proficiency at sniffing out trouble with primitive equipment, remembering that your object is just to get to professional help.

Multipurpose Tools, Pro and Pro

There are some things that fall in a gray area between tools and parts, but which are more often tools. None of them are officially tools, but all are lifesavers. Here are a few:

Wire is used to hold things on or together. You need a dozen feet of a tough, solid-core wire. Don't get braided or laid wire because it won't hold a twisted closure and requires knotting, which is sometimes difficult or impossible. If you have the room, carry twice that much and you will not be sorry for doing so.

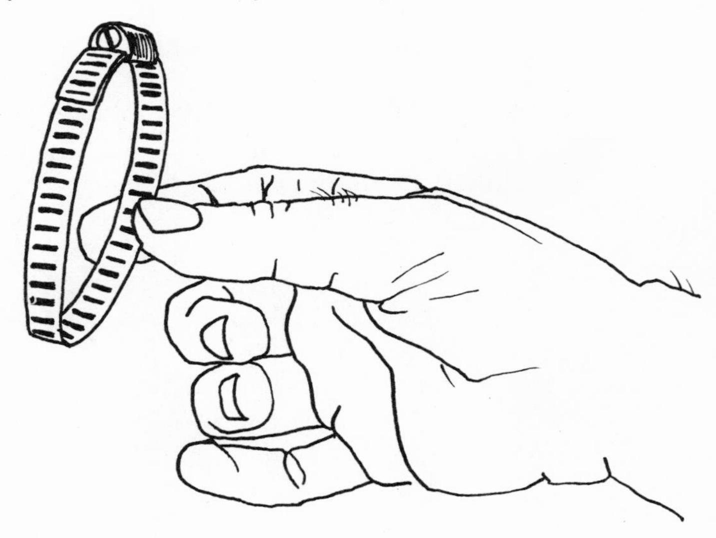

A hose or plumber's clamp.

Plumber's clamps are just about the handiest thing ever invented. They consist of a metal strip with spaced holes over which fits a right-angled screw fitting. When tightened down, a plumber's clamp will hold an amazing tension. I have even seen four of them used to hold a broken *frame* together! They cost about 55¢ each and you can't have too many of them. I take six with me, in two sizes, and have seen times when I wanted two more.

Plastic aluminum, which comes in tubes, is a dull-gray goo that hardens into metal. It costs a couple of dollars a tube and is completely useless until you really need it. I carried some around for three years without using it, then put a hole in my oil pan up in Little Fort, Virginia. The goo sealed the hole so well that I didn't bother replacing the pan for almost a year.

Pocketknife. The world's champion multipurpose tool. No self-respecting kid was ever without one, and no sane biker. Get a plain one of good make and talk nicely to it.

The Indispensables: Spare Parts

Tools are useless without spare parts. It won't help to get that blown tire off if you can't repair or replace the tube.

Tire puncture can be cured two ways: a spare tube or a patch kit. Spare tubes are much surer, but they cost a lot and are a pain to carry around since they puncture easily. (I once stuck a fork through my only spare while it was packed away in the storage system.) Patch kits are slow and require a little proficiency to use, but they are easy to carry. They come in "cold patch" and "hot patch" types, the hot patch being superior. A cold patch goes on with goo, and a hot patch with burned goo, which softens the rubber and make a better seal. Bear in mind, though, that a hot patch requires dry rubber and won't work worth a damn in the rain.

You need to carry spare plugs, spare bulbs for your head and tail lights and for your instrument panel, spare points and condensers, and spare cables. Without any of these, you will be crippled at night, and without most, crippled period.

Sneaky-trick department: cables can be stored by taping them along the cables in use, being sure to tape up the exposed ends to keep grime out. Spare bulbs, points, condensers and other small parts can be taped inside the headlight nacelle of most bikes or to the underside of the seat — up near the front, where you won't crush the bulbs when you sit down.

It's a good idea to carry a package of spare screws, nuts and bolts, and assorted fastenings in the sizes your mount takes. If your make and model of bike has any exotic fittings, carry spares. If it is prone to breaking something specific, carry a spare. If it seems to have a part that's lurking around waiting to sneak up on you some night, carry a spare.

The rule on bike tools and parts is: only as much as you need, but everything you need. Don't try to carry a complete overhaul with you, but don't get stuck for want of a spare cable or a 16 mm socket.

House Tools: How Many, What Kind?

House tools are those you need to function in a civilized manner. They are few in number and simple in design.

First, you need an entrenching tool, which is a military euphemism for a shovel. Since shovels are big and heavy, you need a little one, and the best of them are the tough plastic ones designed for backpackers. You use this tool for digging your fire pit, for trenching around your tent in the monsoon season, and for filling in your latrine like the decent person you are. (Notes on how to be a good guy in camp are in Chapter Sixteen.) The best one made is the EZEE backpacker's trowel, which costs a whole 39¢ and weighs two ounces.

If you plan to spend the major portion of your time in the wilds, you might consider a combination tool made by Kelly. It consists of a small ax, a small shovel, and a small saw, all bound together in a package. The thing costs almost $10 and weighs 5 pounds, and I'd never use it, but a lot of nomads do and swear by it.

A word on axes. The romantic image has the woodsman chopping up his firewood with a hatchet. This won't work. A hatchet is feasible only for small branches, and these burn so fast that you spend all your time trying to feed the fire. A large ax will give you mighty biceps, but will cost you a lot in weight and storage. If you're really into open fires, I'd suggest a folding saw. They take up little room and will produce more firewood for less effort than a hatchet.

The only advantage — and it's a dubious one — to hatchets is that they can be used as hammers. The value is dubious because using a bladed instrument to pound on things is an excellent way to remove your nether appendages.

Still, you need something to drive tent pegs with and to hit your impact driver with. I use my super tire iron because it has a nice, flat end, but that's nearly as dumb as a hatchet. The only solution is a real hammer, and there's not enough use for one to justify carrying it. If you decide to do so, get a plastic or rawhide mechanics' mallet. It will hammer as well as a carpenter's tool and will not damage your pegs or impact driver as badly — nor slip off the striking surface so readily.

Your last house tool is a length of rope of medium strength and diameter. Use this to hang the wash on, to steady the tent in Nepal, and on occasion, doubled and tripled, to tow your mount ignominiously into town. You need 20 feet, but 30 feet is better.

I have not listed the myriad little things like clothespins, sewing kits, dishwashing gear, etc., because you will work out your requirements for yourself, and because the lack of them will pose no serious problems. I have listed here those tools and parts without which your trip might have serious consequences.

I offer here a single piece of wisdom to close this chapter, and it deals with the importance of self-sufficiency on the road.

Wisdom

In February of 1973, a young man's car broke down on a California freeway. He began flagging down traffic.

Eleven hours later, the California Highway Patrol found him beside his automobile, shot through the head. He had left a note that said, "I'm cold. I've tried all night to get help. Nobody would stop. I don't want to live in a world like this."

He had blown his brains out.

10. Medicine

If there is one item common to all nomads it is the medicine chest. No sane traveler is without one. The reason is simple. If your horse — or camel, or motorcycle — breaks a leg, you can still get home. If you break a leg, however . . .

Your medicine chest should be designed to handle emergencies and the more common annoyances. You need not carry equipment for performing brain surgery or for extended treatment of any ailment. The job of your medicine chest is to patch you up sufficiently to let you get to the nearest golf course, where you will find several doctors.

In this chapter we'll look at the contents of the "ideal" nomad's medicine chest and talk about treatment for a couple of common emergencies you can encounter on the road.

Priorities for the Biker

The order of priorities in first aid is different for the two-wheel traveler than for his sedentary friends because his lifestyle promotes a different order of emergencies. Where the city dweller's most common accidents are minor cuts and contusions, the biker's are abrasions and bone breakage. The rate of major burns is greater for house dwellers, but minor burns are more common among motorcyclists. The urban citizen catches more colds, but the biker suffers more cases of exposure, sunstroke, frostbite, etc.

Take a guess at the most common illness among nomads. *Food* poisoning! This happens mostly to the inexperienced traveler who packs a chicken-salad sandwich at night and eats it the next afternoon, but it also happens to the old hands.

So, where the average home medicine cabinet is full of aspirin and Band-Aids, the biker's must contain a more serious selection, and more carefully thought out.

Let's start with the major disasters.

Tools for Treating the Two Emergencies That Won't Wait

Shock and massive bleeding are the prime killers in highway accidents. Shock becauses it destroys the body's ability to fight back, and massive bleeding becauses it robs the body of its most important weapon. In a large number of road accidents, the two conditions go together. Treatment of both must be fast and accurate or the show is definitely over.

Now, we are concerned here only with the actual tools of treatment, and the first of these is your instruction book. This is the tool that tells you how to use the other tools, and it is to be read and mastered *before* it is needed!

First aid book. There are at least a thousand books on the subject of first aid. Most of them are good, a few are dangerously bad, and some are criminal. The best — and one of the cheapest — is the old standby, the *Red Cross First Aid Manual.* It has been around through umpteen reprintings and editions and is the only text besides the army's that has had the full range of human disasters to draw its experience from. It costs about $2 and is available at most bookstores and any Red Cross outlet.

One note on first aid manuals: they all say "take the victim's leg and lift." What do you do if you are the victim? Working on yourself when you are alone and hurt is a whole different game than playing angel to a friend. There is a book on self-treatment in the boondocks and it's called *Being Your Own Wilderness Doctor* by Bradford Angier and Russ Kodet (see the Sources Appendix). Although I have seen it I have never put it to test, but backpackers who have say it's practical.

Bandages, needles, and gut. The second tool you need is a supply of large compress bandages. Not Band-Aids; bandages. These are for blanket coverage of open wounds to staunch bleeding. For minor cuts, linear cuts, and flapping skin, carry a couple of packets of surgeons' needles and gut. These can be bought in a hospital supply house or gotten from your doctor. The latter course is better because the doctor will often give you a demonstration of how to use them. If purchased, they cost about 85¢ apiece.

Antiseptic. Carry an antiseptic, preferably in cream form, for laying over your clumsy stitching and over abrasions and burns. Get a doctor's advice on the composition of the cream because a lot of the commercial preparations do more harm than good.

The rule on shock and bleeding is: treat them fast.

The Secondaries, and What You Need to Treat Them

Most other accidents give you a little time to act before they get serious. Generally, these fall into the categories of breaks and sprains, abrasions, illnesses, and annoyances.

Breaks and sprains are treated by binding and splinting, and by dosing yourself against pain. Your medicine-chest tool for this is a large Ace bandage. Do not carry splints because they take up a lot of room and are easily improvised at hand. The Ace bandage — carrying two is better

— will provide just enough tension to hold a fractured bone in place until you can get to help.

Abrasions are treated with your antiseptic cream, then covered with your next tool, tape and gauze. You don't need more than one large roll of either because really large abrasions, such as those acquired by sliding along the highway on your rump for several yards, can be covered with your compresses.

Illnesses include poisonings, headaches, nausea, and all those internal things that can go wrong with the machine. The commonest of these is Montezuma's Revenge, more widely known as diarrhea.

For illness, you will do best to follow the recommendations in the *Red Cross Manual* and then include whatever medication your own specific system demands. Do you need ointments or unguents for some chronic condition? Carry them. Do you have a tendency toward migraine headaches? Toothache? Athlete's foot? Carry treatment for these things.

If your traveling is mainly of the one-night-camp sort, you can avoid most of these medicines since you won't be more than a few hours away from a drugstore. But if you plan to be back in the hills for a while, take them along.

Generally speaking, your medicine chest should contain the following: headache remedy, toothache remedy, laxative, an antidiarrheal, antiseptic cream, personal ointments, poison antidote.

Annoyances, which means sunburn, bugbites, snakebite, splinters, and things in your eye, are treated with the appropriate tools, all of which are small and available everywhere. Tweezers for the splinter, an eyecup for the boulder under your upper lid, and your favorite nonremedy for the chigger bites. For the snakes, carry a snakebite kit, and it goes *in your pocket,* not in the medicine chest.

A Note on Snakes and Insects

Insects are the real killers of man. They are the dominant species on this planet, outnumbering us, outsurviving us, outwitting us, and even *outweighing* us. Percentagewise, they kill more of us than we do of them. The fact that they do it indirectly, through plague and disease, might be some comfort to somebody, but not to those who die of plague or yellow fever. Each year, insects kill more humans than war, automobiles, and all noninsect-instigated diseases combined.

It is typical of man that he picks the wrong insects to fight. As a race, we carry on a relentless war with spiders. Whatever the official policy, there is something instinctual that causes the individual to stomp on a spider when he spots it.

Yet there are only two spiders in this country that are genuinely harmful to man, the black widow and the brown recluse. Both are quiet creatures who shun man and daylight and will run rather than fight nine times out of ten.

We think of honeybees as "cute" and mosquitoes as annoyances, and these two creatures kill more people than all other insects. We abhor spiders, and they kill more insects than we do.

Snakes bite a lot of lead-footed outdooorsmen. They kill very few. In fact, less than one snakebite in two thousand proves fatal, and then only when treatment is slow or incorrect.

However, snakebite is no laughing matter. A good-sized cottonmouth or rattler is a dangerous animal, perfectly capable of making you that one-in-two-thousand statistic. And any bite by a poisonous snake will make you very, very sick.

There are two distinct types of snake poison, and the treatment for one is often the fatal dose for the other.

This is why it is best to confine your first aid to suction of the wound and a fast trip to the nearest doctor.

Your snakebite kit must be of the "cutter" variety, which is a double-cup suction system made of rubber. It's a couple of inches long, weighs a couple of ounces, and should be on your person at all times. It has a small cutting tool inside, along with a set of instructions that you read as soon as you buy your kit. You do not rely on your scout knife and your own suction for snakebite unless you've figured out how to apply suction to the back of your thigh or your right ear. The cutter kit will reach anywhere and won't leave you swallowing poison.

Finally, your medicine chest needs a small scalpel or a single-edge razor blade, a pair of bandage scissors (they look like a child's shears, short and with rounded points). salt tablets, and a plastic whistle. The whistle is for attracting attention when you're pinned under your mount down in that gully beside the Pennsylvania Turnpike. You can make considerable noise with a whistle, even when you're too weak to holler.

Fit your medicine and first aid tools into something small and sturdy and waterproof. Make it something that you can open one-handed or with your teeth if you have to. Paint it international orange or cover it with reflecting tape so you can spot it if it gets thrown during an accident, and so that passing tourists can see it when you toss it up on the road. (The case — with a help note — not the medicine.)

I carry a small air force signaling mirror in my chest. It has never been called on to save my life, but it's good to shave by.

First Aid Kits

You can buy first aid kits ready-made, and some of them are good buys, if only for the cases themselves. But the selection of tools and medicines is usually hopelessly inadequate or highly optimistic, and you can assemble your own more cheaply. Many contain things like aerosol disinfectant and antiseptic sprays. I'm against them because anything under pressure is a small bomb, and I don't like carrying them around. But they do work and give superior coverage.

Some kits have goodies like fluorescent HELP! signs, which fold up small. I bought a $2 kit just for the sign, once.

The medicine chest should cost $10 to $20. Information: your doctor.

Credentials

First aid goes only as far as you are able to help yourself. In a really serious emergency nothing in your medicine chest will be of value because you won't be able to use it. In this case you have to depend on fate and the passing Samaritan. Fate is notoriously fickle, and Samaria is a long way off both in time and distance — as the last chapter's Wisdom Section showed. But there are a couple of things you can do to load the dice in your favor.

Carry credentials to help the man who stops. Carry credentials to help the ambulance drivers, none of whom are too well trained anyway. Carry credentials to help the doctor avoid fatal mistakes. And most of all, carry credentials that will get you past the front desk. In most larger cities, you'll be taken to a charity or teaching hospital, and the number of people who die there waiting for a doctor is beyond belief. (Note, though, that the doctors in emergency wards are usually the best there are.)

In your wallet, which is the first place the state trooper is going to look, place a folded sheet of bright-colored paper. Put it in one of your plastic picture compartments as near your driver's license as possible — preferably right across from it.

On this paper, on the outside, write EMERGENCY INFORMATION in bold letters. Inside, put your name and address, the names and addresses of (a) your family doctor, (b) your nearest useful relative, and (c) three friends who will accept long-distance calls. Below this, list your blood type, any regular medication you are on, and a very short medical history.

At the bottom, write NOTE! NOTE! and list any allergies or specific conditions that pertain. For instance, "Allergic to tetracycline," or "I am a diabetic." If you have any problem like specific medical allergies or conditions, get yourself a Medic Alert bracelet or necklace and wear it.

And at the very bottom, if you know someone who's good for it, write "Medical expenses guaranteed by ______."

Get yourself some accident and hospitalization insurance and carry your card plainly visible in your wallet. This gets you past the front desk a little bit faster than otherwise. I have talked to several hospitals, and all have said that the only insurance that moves the buzzards on the admissions desk is Blue Cross Group. Unfortunately, most of us can't get the stuff, but any card is worth more than no card.

Finally — and *very* important. Write out a statement authorizing the doctor to take whatever steps he feels necessary to keep you alive. Sign it, have it witnessed and notarized, and carry it folded inside your emergency-info paper. I had a dear friend die because a doctor wouldn't operate without authorization. That piece of paper could have saved her life.

Cajun Road Wisdom

This completes not only your medicine chest but your gear in general. You now have a complete, portable home, the equipment to use and maintain it, and a mount to carry it on. You're ready to saddle up and head out. But . . .

Down in the fine town of Grand Mamou, Louisiana — which is just down the road from Petit Mamou — I have a friend name of Wydell Labourde. Wydell is an over-the-road trucker who's been driving so long he still carries a buggy whip to flog the mules with.

Wydell also rides motorcycles long distances. Once he rode from Lafayette, Louisiana, to Nome, Alaska, on an ancient Harley knucklehead. For this trip, his gear consisted of a World War I leather flying coat, clodhopper boots, a pair of overalls, a screwdriver, one frying pan, a coffeepot, and a steel hip flask full of gin. This was before the superhighways, before the Howard Johnsons and Holiday Inns, and before the days of bike dealers in every town. Wydell made the passage in fine spirits and perfect health, and in three days less time than it took me to do the same journey in 1970.

Wydell supplied the moral to this tale when I took myself down to ask his advice on the book you are holding. He shook his head, snorted, and stated positively that the only tools a biker needed were common sense and a nose for weather.

And I think there's something to that when all is said and done.

PART 2: HIGHWAYS

A highway is . . .

The vein of economy.
A drain on the economy.
An excuse for owning vehicles.
Often beautiful.
A way of proving which towns made it.
A very efficient killing ground.
The most absurd sex substitute yet devised.

11.
PACKING UP

If you take the gear you have assembled for your traveling home out into the backyard and lay it out neatly on the ground, you will swear that there is no possible way to get it all strapped onto your mount. In fact, you would probably have doubts about getting it onto a pickup truck.

But it can be done and fairly easily. Even the most complete home can be put on a trail bike or a 50 cc town-putter, if that is your mount, and this is why: storage systems use the bike as a frame, not an integral component. A saddlebag attaches *to* the bike, so it isn't really important how big or small the bike itself it, except as size affects its weight-bearing ability. If you have stayed reasonably close to the parameters you established with your three-vector systems in choosing your mount and your gear, there will be no problem in loading up.

Every biker who tours has his own packing system, and he knows that it is superior to everyone else's. He also knows that he can improve it still more if only he keeps trying. As a result, there is almost as big a folklore on the proper loading of motorcycles as there was on the proper handling of mules back in the last century. And the subject — like mules — can be discouraging to the newcomer. Even the experienced bike camper might pale a bit when confronted with the sheer mass of a full-scale "house"

spread all over the ground around his bike. I remember that I did.

It isn't simply a matter of sticking everything on the bike and nailing it down. There are a lot of factors that have to be considered. Each item must be looked at from the points of view of its weight and bulk, the frequency of its use, how quickly it needs to be gotten at, how it responds to weather, its breakability, and so forth almost into next week. You would not pack your spare bike parts on top, for example, where you would have to load and unload them each time you needed to get at your spare socks. Nor would you put the eggs on the bottom of your saddlebags, nor your first aid kit under the toolbox, nor the tent pegs in your tank pack, with the tent back on the luggage rack.

Obviously, it's all more complicated than it looks.

To bring order to the packing-up process, establish a

few priorities, then fit your gear inside the resultant parameters. The priorities fall into two categories: external and internal. External priorities deal with the relationship between your loaded bike and the environment, and internal priorities with the relationships among the component parts of your gear. Thus windloading, which means packing to minimize the effects of the wind on your mount, is an external priority, while unitizing, which means putting the tent pegs with the tent, is an internal priority.

External Priorities

They are, in order of importance, weightpacking, windloading, and weatherloading.

Weightpacking is the process of distributing your gear to achieve the best possible center of gravity on your loaded mount (see Chapter One). In theory this means placing your heaviest gear as low as possible on your mount and as near the center of the bike as possible. In actual practice, this can seldom be achieved. There are too many other factors involved. Food, for example, is heavy, but you cannot store it deeply within your system unless you want to unpack your entire home to get at it each night.

Most of the storage capacity of your bike is over the rear wheel and to either side of it. The object in weightpacking, then, it to get as much weight in the bottom of these areas as possible and to *counterbalance* the rest. You counterbalance by loading high-use items with weight (like food, kitchen tools, first aid kit, etc.) *forward* on your mount. If you have wisely decided on a fairing for your mount, you can load much gear inside it. Vetters come with pockets for doing so, but almost any frame-mounted fairing can be rigged with storage areas. (Note: it is not a good idea to put weight on bar-mounted fairings as this will make the handling sluggish and increase the chance of frame oscillation.) If you do not have a fairing, or even if you do, you can utilize a tank pack to help in weightpacking (see Chapter Three). The object in counterbalancing is simply to move the center of gravity of your gear — the deadweight — forward of the rear axle. The ultimate object of weightpacking is to get the center of gravity for the deadweight as close to the center of gravity of the bike itself as possible.

There is a practice to avoid in weightpacking, and this is the temptation to hang things on the forks, the handlebars, or the front fender. Putting either weight or bulk there will severely damage the handling and safety characteristics of your mount. Weight will impede the fork action and bulk will react adversely to wind. Both conditions are undesirable.

Practically applied, weightpacking your mount means keeping things like your tools and spare parts, your bulkier clothing, and your books down in the bottom of your saddlebags, your tent as close to your rump as possible, and as much of the rest of the weight as possible loaded forward.

Windloading means packing your mount so that it won't be blown off the road by your guitar case flapping in the wind. This is a very real consideration and one that the beginning nomad seldom thinks about at all. Partly this is due to myth and romantic images. After all, Peter Fonda ran down the road with his Sears bedroll strapped to a sissy bar, right?

Wrong. Pete ran down the road like that for a few hundred yards: the bikes in *Easy Rider* were trucked from one location to the other.

The rule on windloading is: develop a symmetrical profile and keep it low. Don't strap things to sissy bars; that's just like having a kite built onto the back of your mount. It will push you off the road in crosswinds and turns and will cause you to spend all your time fighting the bike. High loads destroy a machine's ability to track, raise the center of gravity, and are a general bummer. Only in the movies are they romantic and then only for a while.

Another aspect of windloading is packing your gear so that the wind doesn't damage it. Sleeping bags, tents, and othere pieces of fabric gear often come with drawstrings or flaps that will buffet in the wind. In a remarkably short period of time, a 70 mph wind can reduce the strongest stuff-bag or tent housing to shreds.

The solution to this is to tuck all loose strings, flaps, etc., inside, then pack the article so that it presents as little damageable surface to the wind as possible. A sleeping bag, for instance, should have the drawstrings tucked inside, then have the butt of the stuff-bag turned toward the front of the bike.

Colonel Blount's ride. There's a story of a race between a Colonel Blount, who was influential in the settling of Tennessee, and a Creek Indian named Octavius Bluejay for the purpose of proving who had the better horse. Each man chose half the route. Blount, having a strong charger, laid out a straight course along the banks of the French Broad River, near Knoxville. Bluejay, having a small and agile horse, laid out his route through the heavy brush. By race day, all odds were in favor of Bluejay, for the brushy half of the course was considered too rough for Blount and his mare.

But Blount won the race handily by greasing himself and his mount liberally with lard. While this did nothing for the heavier brush, it made enough difference in the lighter stuff to give him the necessary edge to win.

Windloading your mount won't win you any races, but it will show up over the long haul in a safer, more relaxed ride, in better gas mileage, and in extra miles between repairs. The point here being that the *complete* two-wheel nomad, like the complete nomad of history, regards nothing as too unimportant if it furthers the odds of his success.

Weatherloading is the process of packing to minimize the effects of rain and sun on your gear. The object is to avoid discomfort, since most of your traveling home is meant to handle weather without serious damage. Rain or snow won't necessarily damage a sleeping bag, but they will make it pretty uncomfortable to sack out in.

Your house is composed of metal, fabric, and food, in about equal proportions. With consideration given to weightpacking and windloading, most of the metal will shift to the bottom of your storage system, leaving the fabric and food to face the weather. Tools, kitchen gear, and such will wind up being packed in the saddlebags, while your tent and bedroll, your day's groceries, and your weatherskins will all be strapped on top and on the outside. With some items — such as rainsuits — this presents no problem, but what do you do about your bedroll?

Wrap it in plastic. Specifically, in plastic garbage bags. The technique is to place a plastic bag *inside* the bedroll's stuff-bag, then the bedroll itself inside the plastic. You do this because plastic bags will last about five minutes when exposed to the wind, even when tightly tied.

With small items, group several inside one bag, then put the bag inside your saddlebag, your fairing pocket, or some other spot protected from the wind. The rule is: shield your gear from the rain with plastic and shield the plastic from the wind.

Certain things need protection from the sun, also. Optical equipment, for example. If you carry a camera or a pair of binoculars, you'll need to keep them sheltered from the direct rays of the sun. Prolonged exposure to direct light will ruin the optical characteristics of any fine lens, will cause film to reticulate, and will dry out the lubrication in the machine. Since most of us who carry cameras like to keep them handy, the exposure problem is serious. How do you get a rapid shot of that herd of javelina — before they come over and get a shot at you — when your camera is wrapped in a plastic bag and three layers of dark cloth?

There are, naturally, no really good answers to this one. I've seen all sorts of compromise solutions with the emphasis on either protection or rapid use, most of which offered little protection and limited use. You must find your own balance point between these two demands and create your own method of protecting your optics.

I carry my camera in the right-hand fairing pocket, nestled on something soft and covered with my light sweater. The machine can be gotten at rapidly, is protected from the sunlight, and is out of the way. In inclement weather I stick the camera in a Baggie and carry it in my jacket pocket, under my rainsuit.

Internal Priorities

Your next consideration in packing your mount is the internal order of your gear. The factors involved are: use frequency, breakability, accessibility, and unitization.

Use frequency means how often you have to get at a particular item. Your tool chest, for example, can be stored in the very bottom of your system, since it is used infrequently, but you'll have to carry your entrenching tool high, since you'll use it to pitch your tent each night. Likewise, you can store what bulk food you carry — flour, apples, etc. — down deep, even though you must keep tonight's hamburger near the top of the storage system. The rule is: if you use it daily, store it open (on top of the saddle, on the luggage rack, in your fairing pockets, etc.); if you use it every couple of days, store it near the top of your closed storage units; if you use it less often than once every couple of days, store it deep.

Breakability is self-explanatory. You don't put the graham crackers under the tool chest, nor your spare pair of glasses at the bottom of your tank pack.

Accessibility means how fast you have to get at something. The obvious example is your medicine chest. It is a high-weight item of infrequent use and is not particularly breakable. Therefore, it should logically be packed away as deeply as possible under your heaviest gear. But logic fails to tell the story here, since the salient point with your medicine chest is not how often you need it but how rapidly you can reach it when you do.

Unitization means grouping your gear so that all the components of a given system are in one place. This is, of course, not completely possible because of the other factors involved. But it must be thought about now to avoid a lot of frustration later. I know of one biker who kept his silverware in his tool kit, on the grounds that they were tools, and had to unpack his whole rig just to fix dinner. He had been doing this for nearly six months before a lady I was riding with pointed out the decrease in effort possible by sticking the silverware inside his coffeepot. I'll admit that there are few cases that drastic, but almost every rider I know — not excepting myself — has costs himself time and energy by not thinking out which tools go with which systems and then packing them accordingly. It gets a little strained if you try to do it logically. For example, I carry my trowel inside my tent because I use it to drive pegs with. And I carry my toilet paper stuck on the handle of the trowel, because that's the second thing I do when I get off Ganesh after a long day's ride. It sounds dumb in explanation but works perfectly in practice.

What Have You Forgotten?

Once you have weighed all the factors involved and considered each item individually, you will have a fairly good idea of where to store things. Time and experience will show you where you must change and modify.

For practice, and to dredge up that item that has been nagging at the back of your mind, make yourself a couple of lists. Make a list of all your gear, broken down into component systems. Make a detailed list — that's a list of every single thing you are taking. Then make a list showing where you intend to store each item. Do all this before you try to load your mount. Making these lists will not only show you what you have left out of your planning but what you *can* leave out. (Do you really need a canteen?)

Then, after having worked out your storage system on paper, take a deep breath and try to load your bike according to your list. This is always an educational process and usually affords great amusement for onlookers. Never mind the laughter, though; you are going through all this rigmarole instead of just flinging your gear at your mount in order to make your mistakes on paper instead of the highway.

Almost always, you will underestimate the bulk of your gear and overestimate the capacity of your storage units. If you have the patience and sense to approach the loading-up process as I have outlined, you will come to a very realistic knowledge of the physical limits of your mount and the load it must carry, and this is a very, very valuable lesson. You will be following the old Chinese precept that nothing is learned but through experience, and experience begins with test.

As a starting point — and only that — here's how I load Ganesh.

Ganesh has the following storage units:

Side: Two canvas backpacks, each with a large main compartment and two small "outside" compartments.

Front: Vetter Phantom fairing with built-in pockets to either side of the headlight nacelle.

Rear: A medium-sized luggage rack.

Top: In the front, two small compartments built into the gas tank. A plastic map case strapped on with a bunji cord. In back, the rear half of my extrawide saddle.

In the backpacks, layering from the bottom, go: tools and spare parts, divided by weight equally between the packs. Kitchen in the port pack, food in the starboard pack. Weatherskins filling the rest of the compartment. In the outside pockets go livingskins, shoes, gloves, etc., with snacks and quick-fix tools on top (a screwdriver and pliers, etc., for tightening things up).

In the front, my medicine chest, camera, light sweater, face towels, shave kit, and inevitable junk go in the fairing pockets. Maps, writing pad, pen, and envelopes go in the map case. My chain and lock go in the aft tank compartment, over which the map case is strapped, and a plastic bottle of orange juice or somesuch sits in the little forward compartment — which originally held a radio.

In the rear, my cooking grill and flashlight go beneath the luggage rack, and my two bedrolls and my dirty laundry duffle on top of it. These form a cushion for my guitar, which is the bottom item on the rear of the saddle.

On the top, over the guitar, I strap my tent (crosswise), a tripod for my camera, my rainsuit, and whatever odds and ends I want left out for the day.

When carrying a passenger, I leave the guitar and redistribute my top and rear gear thus: A third backpack is added — for the extra gear. It goes on the luggage rack. The laundry duffle still rests on the rack, but the bedrolls move around and sit on top of the side storage units, forming almost an armchair for the passenger. Front and side storage remain the same.

First, Around the Block

Having worked out a system that actually gets all your gear on your mount and still leaves you room to sit down, you are now ready to test the practicality of the rig. You do this, of course, by riding with it.

There are two cautions here. First, start out with half a load and get the feel of that, then work your way up to a full load. Second, try to avoid both heavy traffic and high-speed riding while you are feeling out your mount's response. The reason for both cautions is the same: a loaded bike's handling is radically different from an unloaded one's. You may have vast experience with your mount but you will find it an entirely new machine with all your gear strapped to it. Thus, avoid heavy traffic, where your machine's new awkwardness will be most noticeable, and high-speed runs, where mistakes will more likely be fatal.

The general rule is: around the block until you can do it with ease fully loaded, then a one-day run at medium speed to feel out the quirks, then a weekend run, complete with camping. Whatever bugs there are in your loading system will show up in this series of trials, not out on the rolling plains of Iowa.

When you are thoroughly satisfied that you have a workable house, that you have a packing system that allows you to function properly, and that you are competent riding under a load, make out your will, take a deep breath, and you're off!

12.
RIDING: SUNSHINE

The skills and techniques used to pilot a motorcycle are different from those used to drive a car. They are kin to the skills used in piloting airplanes, in sculpting, in some branches of theoretical mathematics, and in laser-beam surgery. They are, in short, the skills and techniques used for three-dimensional thinking. The automobilist "steers" or points his machine along two dimensions of a three-dimensional track. His options are this-side or that-side, and the road itself takes care of changes in elevation and in the horizontal plane.

The biker, however, lacking the inherent stability of the automobilist's four-wheel stance, must at all times compensate for every change in his machine's relationship to the environment: changes in speed, surface plane, direction, road condition, wind speed and direction. Like the laser-beam surgeon and the sculptor, the bike rider must be able to envision a point in space and time somewhere ahead of him (as in a turn) and calculate a path through all those variables that will bring him to the desired point intact.

With practice, this process becomes so easy it is totally unconscious. The finest computers on earth could not do it so well or so fast as the average biker's brain.

The Interdependence of the Variables

The turn is the basic maneuver in motorcycling, and mastery of turns marks the good rider. A nomad who owns all other touring and riding skills but hasn't proficiency at turns will sooner or later wipe himself out.

The turn is basic because it involves all the variable factors with which the two-wheel nomad contends. It is

also the most common maneuver in touring, being repeated hundreds of times in the average day's ride. Finally, it is the most dangerous maneuver in riding, since a bike that is leaning into a turn loses many of its response options. You can't, for example, swing sharply in the other direction while bent into a turn. Nor can you brake or accelerate rapidly. In a turn, more than in any other move, the success of the action depends on the rider's correct interpretation of each variable, and on his understanding of the interdependence of those variables. If he calculates correctly the centrifugal force acting on his mount, he will maintain his lean without falling over. If he correctly calculates the friction factor of his tires on the road, he won't skid. If he correctly interprets the degree of the curve, he will avoid running off the road. If he does all this correctly and well, and if he *then* miscalculates his speed, or the force of the wind, or the roughness of the road surface and his bike's ability to handle it . . . he will wreck.

Like most precision operations that depend on the immutable laws of physics for their function, motorcycle piloting demands that you get *all* the variables right.

Fortunately, most people who ride motorcycles have both natural ability and some experience with three-dimensional motion, having walked, roller-skated, or bicycled most of their lives. None of which prepare you for the speeds, weights, and forces involved in motorcycle nomadics, but all of which give you a starting point. These skills are mostly unconscious by the time you are old enough to drive motorcycles, and the skills you acquire on your bike will be subliminal and unconscious, too. They are basically manual skills and as such can't be taught on paper. But you can be made aware of the complexity of the process involved and that awareness will help you develop your skills. It will also help you avoid the more permanent beginners' mistakes.

Never assume that you have "mastered" your mount. Never assume that you can become casual about moving down the highway at 60 or 70 mph. Be at ease with your mount, but do not take it for granted. And above all, work for grace and proficiency at the common maneuver, the turn.

Pace and the Long Haul

Of the many riding problems peculiar to the nomad, the most pertinent is pace. Only the long-distance rider has to cope with saddle time measured in hours instead of minutes. The weekender, perhaps, will ride for the better part of a day, but he seldom rides all day for a week or a month, and he doesn't do it with his mount loaded down, either.

There are two problems involved in riding long distance: fatigue and boredom. They are dealt with through pacing, through correct rider position and exercise, and through concentration.

Pacing means developing a rhythm of rest periods and a cycle of activities that promote maximum alertness and minimum fatigue while riding. They key word here is rhythm, for without rhythm no system will work for long. When applied to pacing, rhythm means the intervals at which you either peak or slump, physically and mentally, while riding. You will find that rhythm is independent of your emotional state after a while. That is, you will be more prone to emotional downs at given times, but your riding rhythm will remain basically unchanged. This goes contrary to current psychological thinking, I know, but it holds true nonetheless. I've yet to meet the biker who would be the exception to the rule. Perhaps the thinking would change if we had a few more bike-freak psychologists?

The key to pacing yourself is knowing the distance you intend to ride in a given day or time period. If you are planning to make 200 miles before dark, you will ride a lot differently than you would if you had to put 500 miles behind you.

Knowing your mileage goal, you then set up your

"breaks." A break can be anything from a shift of saddle position to a lunch stop or a siesta. The important part is to have them scheduled. Mind you, the schedule can be as loose as "ride from nine to noon, digging the scenery" or as tight as a military invasion plan.

The object in scheduling your breaks is to give your mind a hook to hang on as the miles go by and to segment the fatigue into manageable chunks. This last point is important. Fatigue blurs the judgment. If you are tired and your butt hurts, but you're trying to make Albuquerque by dark, you'll be tempted to grit your teeth and tough it out, feeling that once you stop it'll be impossible to start again. As a result, you may make an idiot move that you'd never make when rested or *if you knew how tired you were.* Taking scheduled breaks makes it easier to tough it out, since you're only riding for fifteen more minutes, or what have you, and the breaks themselves give you an opportunity to assess how tired you actually are. This is the single biggest lifesaving factor in long-distance riding.

The two types of break are: actually stopping and pattern shifts while in motion. Stopping, of course, is the most complete and relaxing sort of break. But it is also the most demanding in that it requires a lot of energy to crank up again once you're off the bike. Any long-distance runner, any hiker, any swimmer will tell you that after a certain point is reached, the pattern-shift break is the only one that works.

If this sounds contrary to the stress I just placed on the importance of knowing when you are fatigued, remember that the point of all this is alertness, not comfort. If you have no great distance to ride, then by all means ride for comfort. If you must get down the road, comfort is secondary. Like everything else in the book, I'm aiming here to equip you against ultimate problems, not the everyday things.

Stopping can be done in any time span and frequency that suits you, and for whatever reason. But every stop should include a couple of functions. Each stop should include, first, a good, long, allover stretch. A few knee bends and toe touches will do wonders for your circulation, as will a short massage of the backs of your thighs and your buttocks. Do a few waist bends also, with emphasis on the sides and back. The muscles of your lower back take more strain than any other group when you ride.

With these static exercises over, take a short walk to restore all your circulation and to let your body know it's still bipedal. Your internal systems will get a little confused if you don't occasionally perform a couple of the functions they were designed to handle. (A few years ago the navy started a large aircraft carrier steaming in a slow circle. The ship steamed gently round and round all day. By the eleventh hour of circular motion, two thousand of the vessel's three thousand men were down with complaints ranging from upset stomach to inability to see clearly.)

When you've become reacquainted with walking, take an inspection tour of your mount — and really *look* at it. Check for leaks, shifted load, loose nuts and bolts, pieces about to go their own way, the condition of your tires, the tautness of your spokes. I once took a cursory kick at the front wheel of an English machine I had been riding all week and the brake cable fell off the connection! I had inspected the wheel not once but three times in the course of that morning.

Finally, reseat your clothing. Squirm around in your jockey shorts and retuck your shirt. This allows air to circulate and moves the friction points around a little to prevent your rump from becoming raw meat.

These rituals should be performed on *every* break. They can be run through quite efficiently in four minutes, or less time than it takes to gas up. Do them when you get off for the night, before you get on the next morning, and even when you stop only to light up a smoke. Make them a habit and someday they will save your skin.

Change of pace, or the "moving" break, is a way of using physical activity to wake your mind up. The exercise possible on a moving motorcycle is severely limited by the laws of physics and common sense. Mostly you do small isometrics coupled with deep breathing. The effects of this are primarily psychological, except for the breathing, but that's what you're after anyway. It is extremely easy to let the drone of an engine and the heat of a lovely summer afternoon put you into euphoria. Euphoria is a nice place to be, but not when you're traveling down the road. If you develop the habit of timed breaks, the little clock in your head will pull your eyeballs down to your watch on time, and that will pull you back to here and now before you go off into the hereafter.

The actual exercises you can do on your mount will be covered in a moment, under the next heading. For now, though, here is a sample of a short day's pacing.

Goal: 229 miles, Montreal, Quebec, to Albany, New York.

8:30 A.M. Leave Montreal
9:00 A.M. Ten-minute stop, Verdun, Quebec. Gas, tighten packs.
9:45 A.M. Fifteen-minute stop, Barrington, Quebec. Talk to girl, take pictures. Share orange.
10:15 A.M. One-hour stop, Hemmingford, Quebec. Bor-

der crossing paranoias by U.S. customs. Talk to tourists from Belgium.

12:00 P.M. Forty-five minutes at Plattsburgh, New York. Lunch, pick up I-87 south.
1:15 P.M. Moving break.
1:30 P.M. Moving break.
1:45 P.M. Twenty-five-minute stop. Snooze. Pottersville, New York. Gas, kick self for not stopping at Ausable Chasm.
2:30 P.M. Moving break.
2:40 P.M. Moving break.
3:00 P.M. Ten-minute stop. Snack. Glens Falls, New York.
3:45 P.M. Moving break.
4:00 P.M. Moving break.
4:10 P.M. Ten-minute stop. Gas. Malta, New York.
4:35 P.M. Moving break.
4:50 P.M. Moving break.
5:07 P.M. City limits, Albany. Total travel time, 8 hours, 37 minutes. Total *moving* time, 5 hours, 42 minutes.

Note the following things about this trip: the moving breaks occur at an average of every fifteen minutes, becoming a little more frequent toward the end of the day, and the first stop comes a few minutes after the ride started. This stop is to correct all those little things you have set up wrong before they become major annoyances. The theory is exactly the same as the backpacker's — you fix a rucked sock now so that it doesn't give you blisters later.

Note also the short nap I took at 1:45 P.M. I took it less than two-thirds of the way through the day's ride so that getting up again wouldn't require an amount of willpower I might not have. The nap is to relax you all the way through, and is the best therapy for tired rump I know of. Ten to thirty minutes is about right. If you flop out picturesquely enough, especially in a roadside park, you can often attract a free lunch from passing tourists.

Note, finally, the very low average speed I made and the rhythm of my breaks and runs. The effort and strain of piloting your mount goes up almost as a cube factor of the speed you are making. That is, you can waltz along all day at 45 mph with less fatigue than an hour's blasting at 80 mph. The moral here is: drive at the *lowest average speed* that will put you at your destination on time. Juan Fangio, the incredible automobile racer, drove exactly fast enough to stay in front and not a kilometer faster. He not only won more Grand Prix than any other driver in history, but he lived to tell about it.

The major difference between a short day's ride and a long one, believe it or not, is simply an increase in that average speed I mentioned. You will find with practice that you will tend to take about the same number of breaks for the same duration no matter how far you are going. The exception, of course, is that masochistic Vancouver to Los Angeles run that you've just got to try at least once. But in the main, the only change in a long ride will be an increase in the distance between breaks. Times will remain stable. A month after the run I detailed for you above, I had occasion to travel from Willoughby, Ohio, to New York City, which is 501 miles. It took me one hour longer than the Montreal-Albany run, almost to the minute, and required four extra moving breaks and a ten-minute bladder stop in Lock Haven, Pennsylvania. The difference was that on the Willoughby run I cranked Ganesh up to 85 mph and left him there for the duration.

The second aspect involved in combating fatigue and

boredom is rider position and those exercises I mentioned earlier.

How to Sit on Your Mount

In Chapter Three I spoke of setting up your saddle, pegs, and handlebars to offer maximum comfort while placing you in the right position on your mount. The position I advocated was as nearly vertical as possible, with your legs and arms forming right-angle bends. In this position, your back does the least supportive work, your circulation operates most efficiently, and you are most balanced, which facilitates balancing your mount.

However, it is physically impossible — not to mention boring — to maintain a single position all day long, therefore, you shift positions.

Back and forth movement of the body, even a movement of a couple of inches, will change the relationships of every thing about the little closed system that is you and your bike. The center of balance will shift, as will the center of gravity. The machine's responses will alter. Your back will creak into a new set of aches. Your blood will reroute itself. All of which are good temporarily, simply because they offer change.

Legs are the only appendages whose position you can alter significantly while riding. The options are: put them on the rear pegs, put them somewhere forward, put them on the seat. This last, of course, is done only by complete idiots.

The problem with any of the body or leg position alterations is that they interfere with your ability to operate your mount in an emergency. It is difficult to fling your bike sideways precisely to avoid that coyote when you are stretched out along the top of the tank, cracking the vertebrae in your spine.

The rule is: position changes are "short-term" operations. Use them for relief, not for continual operation.

Finally, combat fatigue and boredom with concentration.

Concentration means keeping your mind on the highway. Tests have shown that it takes up to ten times as long to react to an emergency when you are daydreaming. While reaction times are measured in tenths of a second, the difference is still often sufficient to prove fatal.

There is absolutely nothing I can tell you about how to concentrate on the business at hand. I have my own tricks, and so does everyone else, and no two are alike. You will develop your own, and they will either work or you will become a statistic. All I want to do here is impress on you the necessity of learning to keep your mind on the ride.

Wisdom

"*Ride now. Eat later.*"

—Goyathlay, running into Mexico after a raid

"*The wise man studies the stones of the road, for each has a tale to tell of those who have passed before him.*"

—Chinese travelers' saying

"*Three things are foolish: marrying young, eating fast, and riding at night.*"

—English, circa 1100 A.D.

13.

Riding: Rain

The preceding chapter dealt with general riding techniques and the art of pacing yourself. This one deals with how to ride in bad weather, especially in the rain. It is entirely possible to ride all your life without having to make your way through snow or over ice. If you are mostly a city rider, you can even avoid high winds. But if you ride a motorcycle at all, you will sooner or later have to do it in the rain.

Wet Pavement Is to Dry Pavement . . .

Riding in the rain presents only two problems but they are dillies: loss of vision and loss of friction.

Vision loss is dangerous to the nomad because of the speeds and masses involved. If a walker is rain-blinded and falls, he strikes the ground with a couple of hundred pounds of mass, traveling at something under 10 mph. These are figures that the body is designed to cope with. The human skull will usually survive this sort of abrupt change in motion status with nothing more than a lump.

But when the rain blinds you while you are running down the interstate, and you can't tell if that looming shape is a cow, a truck, a boulder that indicates a turn in the road, or a smudge inside your goggles, you have real trouble. The body will not cope with slamming into the

pavement at 60 mph with 600 pounds of bike on top of it.

California, New York, and Kentucky have all run tests on the vision factor in accidents on the road. Their figures are remarkably consistent, showing that loss of vision causes better than 70 percent of all bad-weather accidents. These figures are for automobiles and are concerned mostly with dirty windshields or broken wipers, but the point to be made here is that a motorcyclist loses *more* vision than a car driver. In fact, in a bad rain the biker will lose up to 85 percent of his visual input. That's roughly equivalent to putting three pairs of stockings over your face, a pair of extradark sunglasses, and a box with a small wax-paper window in it over your head, then trying to drive. It sounds absurd but that's about what 15 percent of available light amounts to.

Friction loss means the loss of traction between your

mount's tires and the road surface, and the loss of "touch" on your control surfaces.

The amount of traction your tires lose in the rain depends on a great number of factors, among which are the tread design, the condition of the tires (degree of wear), the type and condition of surface you're running on, the temperature of the air, and the composition of the layer of road grime that your tires actually pass over.

Basically, though, when you are running straight down the road on a set of touring tires in good condition, your traction loss will be between 10 and 35 percent. When the demands placed on the tires rise — as in turns, worsening road surface, emergency maneuvers, etc. — the traction lessens sharply. In a fairly sharp turn, your mount's feet have a smaller "print" on the pavement. This puts more pressure on each square inch of tire surface at precisely the time when it is least affordable.

To the rider who has never been down in the rain this will seem overdone, perhaps, since as long as his bike stays up he doesn't have to consider how precariously it is doing so. But to those of us who have had our mounts literally snap out from beneath us on the slick tarmac — when all seemed so controlled — the figures bear thinking about.

Rainriding was once described as "a lot like ice-skating on a glass lake covered with oiled BBs." That's not far wrong.

The second half of the friction-loss problem only becomes a problem when it's too late to do anything about it. Control surfaces on most motorcycles — that's brake and clutch levers, gearshift and throttle and such — are usually made of metal. Metal, when wet, becomes slippery. And a slippery gearshift lever is not the thing to have under your boot when you have one second to downshift or dump it. This holds doubly true for the clutch.

The problems, then, are simple, if serious. In the rain

your mount becomes willful and precarious, given to capricious behavior and sudden moves along unexpected planes. Your ability to respond is often hampered by poor vision, poor grip, and cold rain down the back of your neck.

What then? Do you sit it out, even though you told the girl you'd be in Denver by day after tomorrow and she's not likely to wait if you are a day late?

No, you ride on. But not the same way you would if the sun were out.

The Importance of Playing Pool

There are two parts to staying alive while rainriding: the mental part and the physical part. The mental involves developing a method of thought, an interior approach, that will keep you ahead of potential disasters.

The process involved is analogous to that used in shooting pool. In the game of pool you win by first making your object ball — achieving the immediate goal — and then *setting up your next shot.* In rainriding, you win by making this curve correctly — achieving the immediate goal — and coming out of it in position for that next curve (or hill or speed zone).

This approach is used in all highway driving, of course, but it is done without thought, and usually sloppily. Watch an automobilist (like yourself, for instance) take a curve sometime. Chances are that car's arc of passage is not as smooth or even as the road, but is instead a number of little corrective maneuvers that take the machine around the curve in a series of scallops. Bikers do the same thing, only not so visibly or so blatantly. But even a little imprecision is too much when riding in bad weather. With so many of the odds going against you, you don't need to contribute any of your own.

Thus, the rainrider must not only plan his "shots" with

more care than when riding in the sunshine, he must also execute them with greater precision.

Just as a pool player must recalculate his angles after a table has been resurfaced or rerailed, the rainrider must recalculate all those thousands of bits of information and experience that tell him just how fast he can take a given hill or just how to approach a gravel road. In the rain, man and mount become much closer, for the nerve endings are nearer the surface.

There are some generalizations that help.

Why You Don't Ride Down the Center of the Lane

The physical part of staying alive in the wet involves knowing the limitations of your mount, the true condition of the surface under you, and some sneaky tricks gathered from survivors. The first two parts of that statement are not open to discussion because they are subjective judgments, things that you will have to decide for yourself. No one but you can "feel" the road beneath your mount for you. No one but you can tell when your bike is on this side of the ragged edge of dumping.

But the third part . . .

Rule: practice dropping your bike a couple of times on wet grass. Do this at a low speed and you'll not even scratch the paint. You are not doing this to learn how to drop the machine — that's covered later — but so that you will *know* what it feels like. If you've never done it, you will be astounded at how jolting a 3-mph spill can be.

Rule: never ride in bad lightning storms. Many of the people who are killed by lightning are killed on motorcycles.

Rule: don't ride down the center of the lane; that's where oil collects and it all comes to the surface during a rain. This is particularly true on city streets, where cars stand and drip at the stoplights.

Rule: gently try your brakes at least every three minutes when rainriding — to dry them out.

Rule: never pass a truck in a rainstorm unless you can keep one full lane between you. This is because he can't see you for his own spray, even with your lights on.

Rule: allow four to five times the stopping distance you would allow on dry pavement. (This is pool tactics.)

Rule: always remember that you can travel just as fast on a wet road as you can on a dry one — as long as nothing goes wrong. But the faster you are traveling when you make your mistake, the more brutal the lesson you will learn.

Moral: common sense and a 30-percent reduction in your over-the-road speed will make you less likely to collect on your insurance.

Rainrigging

To prepare yourself and your mount for rainriding — or any bad weather for that matter — do the following:

Make sure your gear is stored properly, that it is weatherproofed, and that everything is tied down well. Wet gear will tend to slip and slide, and that will have a deleterious effect on your survival.

Check the little obvious things on your mount, like the gas cap being on tight and the high-tension spark-plug cables being well insulated. Conking out in a downpour is not a happy-maker.

Look to your treads and pick out any accumulated rocks or other matter. You'll need all the traction you've got.

Check all your control surfaces. A note on this: if you don't have rubber gripping surfaces, tape your lever ends with your black electricians' tape. (You did get the good, gooey black stuff, didn't you? Not that shiny plastic tape!)

Now, defog *all* your vision surfaces. That means your eyeglasses, your goggles, your face shield and your windscreen — or whatever combination you have. The rule is: the closer to your eyes the surface, the more urgent the need for defogging.

Your fairing's windshield will seldom fog, especially if you keep it polished with one of the plastic polishes made for windscreens. But your face shield will, and so will your goggles. You can cure this with any of the commercial preparations made for race drivers and scuba divers or with a much cheaper preparation of one part banana oil to three parts cooking oil. Make yourself a little squirt bottle of the stuff and carry it somewhere in your raingear unit — like the pocket of your rainsuit. A couple of drops on the lenses of glasses or goggles, spread around with your finger, will smooth out into a nonblurry, nonfogging coating that will last for several hours. You'll smell like a banana salad for a while, but that's nice, too.

Next, button yourself into your rainsuit. Check all the vents to see that your body can breathe properly. Check your closures for watertightness, paying special attention to the neck closure and the area around your boot tops. If you have equipment that goes over your boot tops, make sure it will stay. If your weatherskins don't include waterproof bottoms, haul out those plastic garbage bags you've got. Poke two leg holes in one and wear it like a large diaper. Wrap two more around your feet over your socks and under your boots. Put your boots on, pull the bags up, pull your pant legs down over the boot tops and strap them there with rubber bands, clothespins, a couple of feet of your wire from the tool chest, or your extra bootlace.

My fairing has one flaw: it is so designed that all the water that it keeps off my tender body flows down the fairing and floods onto my boots. Inside of half an hour, my feet feel as though they've been wading in the Arctic Ocean — this in spite of being perfectly dry inside. The lesson being that you *must* pay particular attention to your feet in bad weather because there are so many odd factors working to make them — and you — ill.

When you and your mount are properly rigged, crank up and let your machine get warm. Let yourself get wet all over and check for leaks. None so far? Okay, turn on all your lights, with your headlight on bright, turn your pipe upside down, and move out.

When riding without a fairing, keep your head as low as possible without crouching, which puts your body in a bad position for emergency motion. If you haven't a face shield, you will be limited in both the speed you can make and the duration of your ride because your face will get eaten off by the rain. At 50 mph there's little difference between a raindrop and a rock when it hits your nose.

If you have no eye protection, do not ride in the rain.

I have eyeglasses, over which I wear a flat face shield, and in front of which I have my windscreen. By process of much trial and error I have gotten the windscreen adjusted so that rain sails over my head when I'm sitting correctly, and my face shield adjusted so that water blowing up through the fork opening in the fairing gets me in the chest instead of the face. Consequently, I can ride through a fairly heavy downpour with only an occasional drop striking the face shield and nothing at all reaching my face. This gives me far better survival odds than the unprotected or poorly protected rider simply because I can see!

I have found that bad weather will cut your day's range by about 40 percent. That is, if you average 300 miles a day in good weather, you will average 180 in the rain.

You can beat this, of course, but at the cost of your fatigue safety margin.

Wisdom

"Come to terms with your ass, for it bears you."

— The Bible

14.

ALL FALL DOWN

This chapter deals with disasters, how to avoid them, and how to handle those you can't avoid. I define "disaster," for this chapter's purposes, as a moving violation of the laws of physics. That is, doing something that disobeys the rules of motion. This includes traveling too fast for a given surface, overestimating your traction, leaning too far in a turn, etc. Anything, in other words, that will have horizontal consequences.

There are two classes of "fact": those arrived at by general consensus and those not subject to human conceit. For example, we all know that "up" is a given direction. But it is that direction simply because we have all agreed to call the direction by that sound. "Gronk" or "flivel" would do just as well, as long as we all agreed on its meaning.

The second class of fact is illustrated by the existence of gravity. Gravity will continue to pull stones down no matter how many of us deny its power to do so, its right to do so, or its very existence.

It is important to understand the difference between these two classes of facts, for disaster most often comes as a result of confusing the two.

The Instinctive Disaster

A good illustration of the foregoing involves the difference between steering and turning. Since we were old enough to consciously pick directions, we have each been conditioned to "steer" right to "go" right. You turn a car's wheel left to go left, you pull a wagon's tongue right to go right, etc.

But on a motorcycle, the exact opposite is true. If you push your mount's handlebars to the left, you will move to the right every time. By the time you have ridden a motorcycle for five miles, you will have learned that you steer a bike by leaning it, but in an emergency situation, nine bikers out of ten will at least momentarily revert to instinct and shove the bars in the direction of escape.

The second form of instinctive disaster is the light that comes on in your head in an emergency and yells *stop!* at you. In an automobile, this is usually a good policy, but on a machine that operates on gyroscopics and centrifugal inertia — like a motorcycle — emergency braking more often contributes to the disaster than alleviates it.

The third form of instinctive disaster is common to all people and all emergencies: freezing up. The immobilization of the body in an emergency probably kills more people than it saves, even though it worked perfectly when it was invented. (What else can you do when faced with a sabre-tooth cat but freeze and hope he's nearsighted?)

The second class of disasters is the mechanical. These include blown tires, no brakes, clutch malfunctions, fire, etc.

The final class of disaster is the outside, or it-wasn't-my-fault variety. In this group fall the wandering cow, the oncoming drunk, the piece of the West Virginia Turnpike that fell down the mountain an hour before you came around the curve, the ten-car pileup that you happen to be in the middle of, and like situations.

Of the three forms, the first, or instinctual, is almost always avoidable, the second can be made infrequent, and the third is beyond your control save for the sanity of your riding habits.

You avoid the first kind of disaster by being alert, by knowing the difference between the demands of physics and the urges of your instincts, and by practicing the correct responses.

You avoid mechanical disasters by vigorous maintenance of your machine and prompt attention to any complaints it offers you.

You avoid the third by riding defensively and hoping your luck holds.

But with all the luck in the world, the best maintenance, and superb training, you might still have to contend with a hard choice somewhere up the line.

How do you handle a disaster when it comes?

Common Effect

Moving disasters for the biker can be classified by their effect, which is much more important than their cause. It matters very little whether a beer-can, a blown tire, or an oil slick has caused you to lose traction; the thing you must cope with is a falling bike.

In this way, we can classify disasters into a few "effect" groups and show you how to handle each class.

Here are the classes:

Falling down at speed
Falling down slowly
Seizures
Brake loss
Power loss
Confrontation
Fire

Almost every moving disaster fits into one of these broad categories, and each category has a specific reaction procedure.

Falling Down at Speed

There are two situations in which you will put your bike down when traveling fast. First, when you have no choice at all, and second, when dropping your mount is the better of two choices. Having no choice means something like blowing the front tire. Having a choice means when you can't possibly avoid that hay wagon in front of you. The approaches to the two situations differ somewhat.

The object, when you have to drop your bike, is to get out from under it. That's all. *Not* to try to "ride" it, not to try to aim it somewhere; not to try to salvage something besides your skin. Simply get yourself from under the bike. The reason is plain. If your leg is scooting along the pavement, you will lose skin. If it is scooting along with a few hundred pounds of bike on it, you will lose meat. All you are trying for in a high-speed drop is survival.

Here is a place where instinct will kill you. When you fall, your instinct is to put out your hand or foot to stop yourself. If you do this on a fast-running bike you will most often break the appendage and yank yourself off the machine in an uncontrollable position. What you work for in a fall situation is to place yourself on the ground, behind the bike, on your back, with your feet aimed in the direction of your slide. You try to keep as much of your body surface in contact with the ground as possible to distribute the per-inch pressure and to slow your slide at the maximum rate. You will lose more skin this way, but less deeply. You keep your feet toward the slide, or the potential point of impact, to put as much mass between that point and your head as possible.

The correct technique for getting out from under a falling bike is to pull both knees up until your feet clear

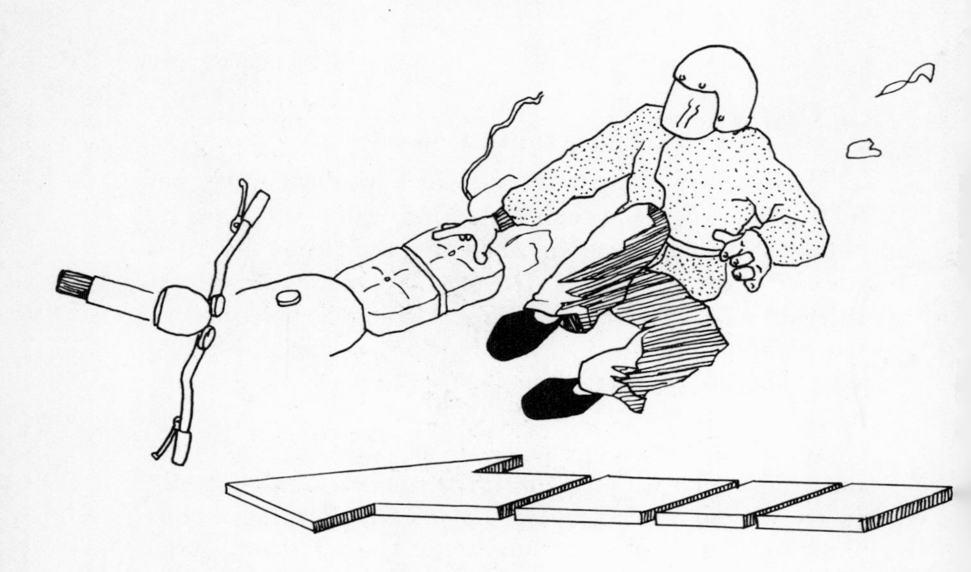

Dropping a bike at high speeds.

the engine casings, put your hand on the saddle or frame on the side of your mount *opposite* the direction of fall, and push yourself away sideways as the bike goes down. You attempt to hit the pavement with your feet, your butt, and your palms simultaneously, and stretch out backwards immediately. Don't dig your feet in first or they will catch and cartwheel you. Likewise, if you come down hard on your hands you will break both arms at the shoulder.

As this sort of accident usually happens with great speed, you never have time to think all this out consciously. Therefore, practice it beforehand. Not the falling, but the tucking motion, which goes so counter to your instinctual reaching motion.

Dropping your bike when you know you are going to hit something differs in that you attempt to keep the machine between your body and the object. You do this by

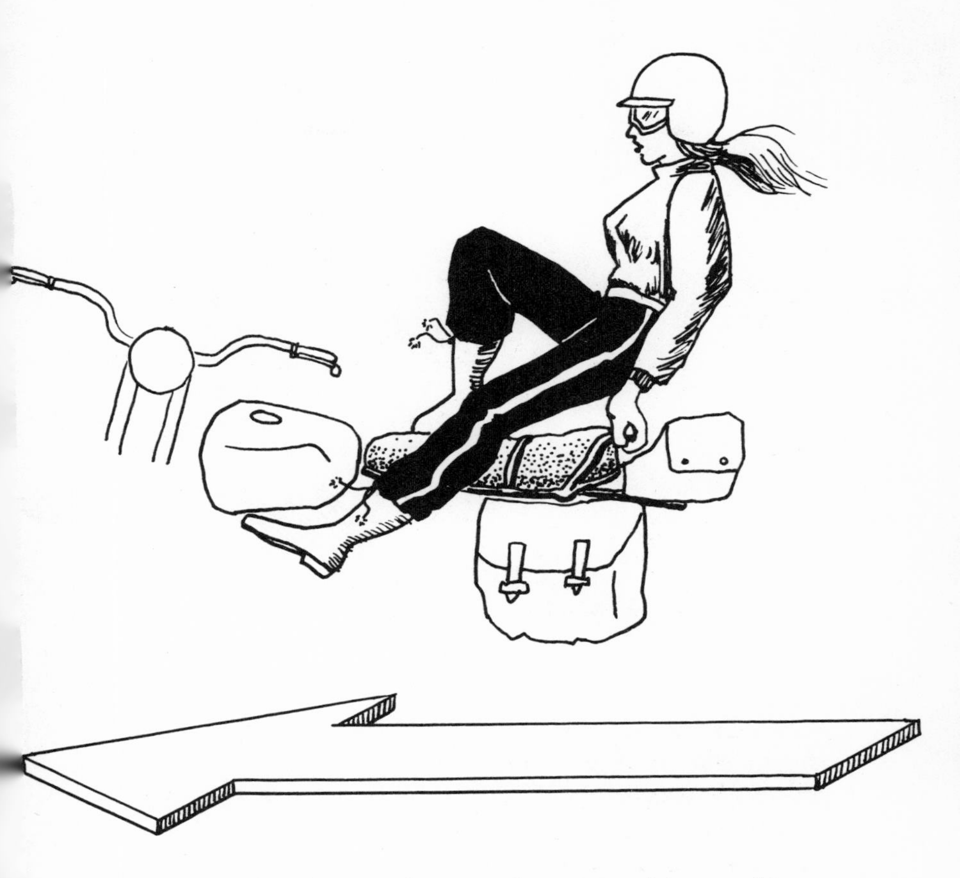

Dropping a bike when you know you're going to hit something.

grasping the *rear* of your saddle instead of the side and propelling yourself off backwards.

Goin' Down Slow

Dropping your bike at low speeds involves a whole different approach. It can often be done without even scratching the paint.

At any speed under 20 mph, on a relatively smooth surface, you can ride your mount down and stay on it

Dropping a bike at low speeds.

until you come to a stop. The technique is the same as dismounting a horse. You stand on the offside peg, hold the bars, and swing your leg out from under the fall. You will probably get a few burns from hot casings and such, but even this can be avoided in most cases. It is possible to ride your mount down because at slow speeds a bike will tend to swing its rear section around as it drops, which dissipates a lot of energy and sets up a centrifugal thrust that helps keep the bike from flipping or end-for-ending once down.

The object in a low-speed drop is correct assessment of the potential danger, so that you can know whether to try to save yourself from skin burns or play it safe and try for pure survival. When in doubt, risk your skin and save your bones.

The next class of moving disasters is seizures.

Seizures

A seizure occurs when the engine, the rear wheel, or both suddenly freeze up and refuse to turn. The two causes of this condition are piston seizure in the engine — particularly in two-stroke mounts — and broken drive chains. The effect of the former is more costly but less sudden. A frozen engine will almost always take a few seconds to grind to a halt. This not only gives you some reaction time, it slows the bike down a little. And in a disaster situation, 3 mph can make a vital difference. A snapped chain, however, if it locks the rear wheel, will do so instantaneously. That means in about one-tenth of a second.

In either situation the danger comes in the rapidity of the change in your mount's status. There is nothing wrong with slowing down unless you do it in a tenth of a second!

The prime reaction your mount will have is a loss of traction at the rear wheel, due to the lockup. This has the same effect as skidding on ice or oil and is compensated for in the same fashion: by careful steering and much prayer.

The secondary concern is that your tire will blow. At any speed over 5 mph a blown tire is serious. At freeway speeds it can be fatal. This is especially true of the nomad's mount, for it is more heavily laden than other machines. This has a double-edged effect: the rear end reacts more slowly because of the extra mass, but once in motion is harder to stop. That means you'll have that eye-blink's grace before the rear end starts coming around, but once it does it will be a juggernaut.

The object in any seizure is quick reaction to the steering problem and controlled loss of speed. If your engine has seized, pull in your clutch and brake down. If your rear tire seizes, chances are the engine will stall out anyway. If not, clutch it in and *stay off the front brake*. With a loose and mobile rear end, the last thing you want is radial back pressure from the front end. A locked-up rear wheel will stop you quickly enough.

Brake Loss

Brake failure is not a common thing but it does happen. Most often it is caused by moisture in the brakes, overuse (fading), or snapped control cables. It has happened to me twice and both times in potentially hairy situations. The first time was in city traffic in Los Angeles, when I sailed right through a red light onto rush-hour Santa Monica Boulevard, and the second was coming down a long mountain in Vermont.

In the first instance I gritted my teeth, closed my eyes, and screamed. I'm told that I missed everybody by at least an inch, and some cars by nearly three. Having since thought a lot about this occurrence, and having talked to other riders, I conclude that what one should *not* do is try to steer into the traffic flow — which was what I first thought of. Reason is that you have less than twenty feet of width in the average two-lane city street. At a mere 5 mph, you *can't* turn a heavy bike in that space safely. The alternatives are (a) that you drop the bike and get ground into hamburger by the oncoming traffic, or (b) that you overshoot the lane and run head-on into the traffic moving in the other direction, getting turned into red grease in the process.

The best advice I can give is to lean on your horn, aim straight across the intersection, and lift the leg on the side the traffic is going to hit you from. If you have that leg up you'll not only save it from being minced, you'll be more likely to be thrown onto the hood of the car that creams you rather than out into the street for the other cars to play with.

Brake loss on a long grade is as dangerous as the country you're passing through. This is because you often have to depend on the land itself to stop you. When Ganesh lost all anchors coming down Prospect Mountain in Vermont, I was faced with a 3-mile grade made of switchbacks, loops, and long open glides. For most of the way there were rocky banks and trees on either side, with open falls in some spots. Not the ideal place to have to ground a bike.

The first move you make when you've lost your brakes is to downshift. On anything but a really long or really steep grade you can *always* reduce your speed to manageable proportions this way. But on something like Prospect Mountain, with almost 1000 pounds total weight to hold back, the engine wasn't enough. By shifting down, then letting the speed grind back up, then shifting down again, trying always to keep Ganesh at something under 40 mph, I put 2 of the 3 miles behind me, continually hoping for a flat spot, a soft spot, or somewhere to rub against.

But luck was not there. The last mile was flatter but it was residential, leading into the town of Bennington, and I could not see hurtling through the city streets like an escaped hippo, endangering children and milk wagons.

The two options left at that point — and these are common to most grade brake-loss situations — were dropping Ganesh or rubbing him. The difference is one of plane. Dropping puts your mount horizontal. Rubbing keeps it more or less vertical. I chose to rub. This means running your bike along the curb, if there is one, or through brush, if there is any handy, or into anything that will impede your speed without wrecking you. Any of these maneuvers is tricky and will fail more often than it works, but all are preferable to slamming into something or somebody full tilt.

Lacking any of the rubbing materials above, I took Ganesh into the ditch on the mountain side of the road. This put him in a rough, boulder-strewn, V-shaped trench, trapped between the high roadbed on one side and the mountain on the other.

It took almost 50 yards to stop, during the course of which both tires blew, the fairing cracked on the right side, I was thrown off and sprained an ankle, and one mirror was broken.

But stop we did, and machine, nomad, and passenger all came out with frames, engines, and major accessories intact, which would not have been the case if we had plowed into the city of Bennington out of control.

The object, then, in brake-loss situations, is to reduce speed and find a method of stopping yourself that promises as much control as possible.

In most brake-loss situations on the road, you can usually coast blithely to a stop unharmed. From the data I've gathered, the two-wheel nomad most often discovers his lack of anchors as he pulls onto an off ramp from a freeway or interstate. He is usually doing something like 50 mph when this happens and has about an eighth of a mile to stop in. He usually has good vision, often has a stretch of road ahead of the ramp to use, and nearly always has grass to dump in if he has to.

Power Loss

Power loss is a common problem on the road, but it is seldom an emergency consideration. When it is, however, it can't be treated lightly. If you're in the middle of a fast-moving traffic pattern, surrounded by several hundred tons of trucks, cars, and people, the sudden loss of motive ability can be very dangerous. Particularly since there is usually no external signal of your sudden deceleration to alert that dozing guy behind you, as there is when you put on your brakes and activate your stoplight. The first thing he sees is your tailpipes moving back at him.

Another situation where power loss is dangerous is in turns or on grades; in fact, anywhere that the physics of your mount's situation requires smooth power to maintain status. If that power fails, the balance of forces fails and you must make adjustments in your turn. This is fine unless you happen to be going up or down some of the hairpin roads in Yugoslavia where there isn't anywhere to adjust the turn to!

There are countless ailments that can cause power loss, so your first consideration in handling this emergency situation is to avoid speculating on what went wrong. *Don't* start peering between your legs trying to ascertain the source of your problem; you'll acquire several more that way. Look *first* to your surroundings, like a pilot looking for an open field. Pick a soft spot to land in, check the traffic around you, signal your intentions loudly and clearly. Then move with what dignity you can muster to the safety of the roadside. And that means as far off the road as you can get. Next time you find yourself on the shoulder of a road, look at it closely. You'll find that there are tire tracks all over it, and on the nearby ground as well. When you're stopped on the shoulder, remember those tracks and note that all of them were made by something running through the space you are currently occupying. It is gruesome how many people get killed while standing or parking on the shoulders of highways.

The next emergency is often the worst: confrontation.

Confrontation

This means hitting something, or nearly hitting something, the object being to avoid it if you can or to handle it if you can't.

In almost all cases of confrontation, the motorcyclist is free of blame. The biker is the victim rather than the aggressor. This is not much comfort when you have just been mangled.

However, it points up the most salient characteristic of motorcycles: they are invisible to other drivers. Better than 60 percent of all confrontations involving a bike happen because the offending party really did not see the two-wheeler. Of the rest, most are misjudgments on the automobilist's part, stupidity on the biker's, and a small percentage of deliberate actions by ugly folks.

But we are more interested here in the kinds of confrontation you must deal with than in their causes. Statistically, they break down as follows:

Side collisions	55 percent
Frontal collisions	13 percent
Rear-end collisions	22 percent
Stationary collisions	10 percent

Most confrontations involve the biker being struck from the side. Most often this occurs in traffic, and most often it is the result of someone running a light. Many times, however, it results from that invisibility bikes have in the automobilists' eye. Gordon Graham, the blues musician, was riding along Sunset Boulevard, going east in the inside lane, when a lady in a Mustang — running east in the outside lane — simply cut across his bows in a left-hand turn. She had neither seen him nor signaled and was profuse in her apologies, which she tendered while Gordon lay on the pavement with bones sticking through his calf.

Most frontal collisions are caused by the biker running up someone's tailpipe. I don't know how many of these accidents are the result of people stopping suddenly and how many of the biker not stopping suddenly enough, but all are the result of the biker not being prepared for the possibility.

Rear-end collisions most often involve drunks running up your fender. There are a lot of these accidents, but they are less often fatal than any other class of confrontation. I think that this is due to the lack of a seat back on motorcycles, which prevents whiplash and that whole list of neck and head injuries. Of course, being plastered all over the grille of a Trailways bus is not that healthy.

Stationary confrontations involve the biker hitting something that isn't attacking him, such as a tree or a house. In a few cases, this is an option that the biker takes to avoid hitting something else — a person, a truck, etc. But in most instances, the cause is stupidity on the biker's part. Since collisions with stationary objects are almost always head-on, the rate of fatality and serious injury is exceptionally high.

There is no real way to "handle" confrontation emergencies other than to avoid them. The only defense is defensive driving, riding as though everyone and everything around you were an enemy just waiting for the opportunity to do you in severely. And in the ultimate sense, this is so. It has been so for every traveler in every land throughout history. Nomadics has been described as the process of finding new and interesting ways to get killed, and this, too, is so. Nothing in all of man's history is as deadly as a highway, and the two-wheel nomad must always bear this in mind, lest he become a statistic.

The object in confrontation emergencies — if you cannot avoid them — is to put as much mass as possible between you and the thing you're going to confront. Try to keep any hands and feet and such out of the area that is going to be folded, spindled, or mutilated and attempt to keep your head clear of hard surfaces.

None of this is usually possible in a confrontation because of the speeds involved in catastrophes. But a knowledge of the correct procedures might give you a fractional margin of reaction.

The final disaster is very rare: fire.

Fire

This happens suddenly on bikes, and most frequently in gas stations. In this case, run for the extinguisher that the law requires the station to have. If you can't get it and get back in 6 seconds, run like hell.

If the fire occurs while you are riding, *Stop! Get off the bike! Run like hell!* Almost always, a bike fire can be put out safely. But if you get unlucky and pick that wrong time, you will go up in a large ball of flame. I have seen this happen, and no bike is worth risking it. Your tendency is to stand about 6 feet away and lean gingerly toward the bike, tossing sand or waving a blanket. But when a friend's Harley went up, the explosion charred the paint on a parked car 15 feet down the street and the leaves off a tree 20 feet back from the sidewalk. Not "burned" or "singed"; *charred.*

The Three Most Common Accident Situations: How to Avoid Them

I've covered the disasters of bike nomadics here, but there are a few little things that happen with much greater frequency than the bonebreakers, and which you will probably have to contend with early on in your career. None are catastrophic but all are annoying and potentially dangerous.

Here are the three most common danger situations and how to avoid them.

Traffic lights. Half of all minor accidents happen at traffic lights. Some are sillies — like falling over when you stick your foot down in a greasy patch — and some are serious — like getting hit by a light runner. Most can be avoided by common sense and timing. Common sense means recognizing that you are in the most dangerous situation you can find on the roads and acting accordingly, and timing means understanding that most intersection accidents happen in the first couple of heartbeats after a change of lights. Your defense behavior centers around doing nothing drastic during those "beats." Don't gun out into the intersection the instant the light changes. Don't try to beat the caution light. Don't assume that the intersection is clear just because there's nothing in it as you approach it. And watch out for pedestrians, who cause about half of all traffic-light accidents. They'll walk on the red light, creep across like snails, flash into view on roller skates and bicycles, and all without any notice to the approaching biker.

Parking lots get more than a few two-wheel nomads. Long-distance riders do a lot of parking-lot driving since they shop for their food in the cities, and usually at the chain stores. And a chain-store parking lot is only slightly safer than a dodge-'em-car track at the fairgrounds. You can get hit more ways in a parking lot than anywhere else. I even know a lady who got hit from above! A kid threw a sack of groceries on top of his VW; it sailed over and clouted the biker square in the head.

In parking lots, ride as though you are the Indians and it's Wounded Knee. They're all around you and they're out to get you. I had a woman miss me once and back up to get me again in a parking lot! She had almost clipped me as she rushed to the street exit, then changed her mind and *backed* into the parking lot. I was on a little Honda 175 cc with a big lady named Sandra, and the woman's car just plowed us under as I sat there stupefied with disbelief.

Driveways, and the process of getting into and out of them, get a lot of motorcyclists. I think the main reason is that you don't really turn your head on until you are out there in the traffic, and the driveway is something like an interim system that doesn't count.

But it does count. Anything counts when it can hurt you.

The usual problem with driveways is the things people leave in and around them: tricycles, garden hose, toys, gravel, etc. Also, they are often fenced with parked cars, which will render you invisible to that sleepy driver coming down the street. You can see him okay, so you pull out, judging that he'll pass easily. But *you* appear like Banquo's ghost; you startle him, he swerves, and there is an accident.

All Fall Down

There are a couple of things going in your favor if you are rigged as a true bike nomad. Your mount will offer you more protection than the average rider's machine because it is heavier and because of the way it is accoutered. The fairing, particularly if it is frame-mounted, and the packs or bags of your side storage system will serve to cushion the bike's fall. More importantly, they will keep the body of the machine off the pavement, and thus off whatever portions of your anatomy you haven't been able to get out from under the machine.

The very bulk of a road-rigged mount makes it more visible and gives the car driver a stronger awareness signal. It makes you more substantial in his consciousness.

But none of these things will help in a bad-luck situation. The best riders sometimes fall down, and every now and again some of them don't get up. Keep in mind as you ride that you are playing a potentially deadly game, and that the ultimate stakes are your life.

15.
Troubleshooting

There will always come a time, no matter how good your luck, when your mount sighs and gives up on you for no apparent reason. This chapter deals with how to determine why your beast went on strike, what to do to persuade it to run again, and how to behave if it won't.

Care and Feeding

At a rough guess, I'd say that less than 5 percent of all bike troubles are unforeseeable. The other 95 percent happen because of sloppy maintenance, poor judgment, and downright stupidity. Cables don't snap unless they are badly frayed in the first place. Tires with good tread don't blow out unexpectedly. Engines with correctly adjusted oil flow do not seize.

I have made the point earlier in this book that maintenance and tender loving care will do wonders for both you and your machine. I make it again and tell you another value in keeping your mount in good shape: when something quits on the road, you can eliminate a lot of things right off the bat. If you keep up with your oil's condition, changing it on schedule and checking it during your stops, you'll *know* that your problem isn't in the oil or its functions.

Along with proper maintenance, there is a lifesaver you can perform before you set out on the road. Memorize your mount's owner's manual and the shop manual I recommended that you get when you bought your mount. Not "read," mind you; memorize. You cannot assess whether your engine's overheating is due to the plugs being too hot if you don't know the correct gap for the plugs. And you can't time the bike without knowing how many degrees off top dead center the cylinder fires. The rule is: the more you know about your mount's innards, the more likely you will be to get it moving again when it quits in the desert.

The best way we have yet found to solve problems is the structured approach, wherein you take a logical progression from point A to point B, testing and eliminating one factor at a time. Surgeons use this approach in exploratory cutting; mathematicians and logicians use it in solving equations; engineers use it in figuring stresses. In fact, all professionals use this method — including mechanics.

But the average nomad approaches his mount when it sits malevolently broken as though it were susceptible only to magic and threats. He walks around it, kicks it, curses and wheedles it, and tries all the controls as though the wish would bring his machine back to life.

In about the same amount of time all that takes, a man following the analyze-and-correct rituals can usually determine what's wrong with the machine, and often have it running again.

The two prime rules of troubleshooting are: know your bike before you *have* to know it and follow a logical sequence when diagnosing. Neither will guarantee that your mount will respond, but a lack of either can guarantee that it won't.

Procedure One: Get Off the Road

Correct procedure starts the instant you notice something wrong with your mount. The first procedure is a "don't," and it is: don't start eyeballing the engine while bombing down the freeway. As I've mentioned before, this can get awfully fatal.

So, clutch in, check traffic, get well off the road. There are two reasons for doing this. First, no matter how minor the requisite repair, you won't be able to do it while mounted, and second, you can use the coasting time to begin analyzing your trouble. How did the engine quit? Did it just stop running, or lose power, or cough and sputter? You can tell a great deal about your problem from the way your beast died.

Procedure Two: Dismount and Unpack Your Tools

Do this instead of walking around the bike looking for what's wrong. This allows you to get over your self-pity and anger at the unfairness of the situation, gives you something physical to do while you calm down, and will make the repairs go much more smoothly — you won't have to get up and rummage in your pack every time you need a tool.

Procedure Three: Diagnosis

Lay your tools out neatly, squat down, and think about what happened. Starting with the really stupid things, here's how you begin diagnosing:

Engine quit suddenly. Loose wire in electrical system. Kill switch accidentally moved to off position. Broken wire or connection. Fuse blown.

Engine coughed and sputtered before quitting. Loose wire. Fuel starvation. Check gas tank, fuel lines, carburetors.

Engine runs but no power. Chain broke or jumped the

sprocket. Clutch worn or out of adjustment. Broken main shaft key. Transmission break. Broken internal springs or cables.

Engine slowed, then quit. Possible seizure, particularly in two-stroker. Fuel impediment. Clogged carburetor or air cleaner.

Engine smoked heavily as it quit. Burned valve. Holed piston. Oil feed out of adjustment (two-strokers).

Engine made expensive noises as it died. Broken internals, pistons, valve, gear or shaft in transmission, rod, etc.

You have three kinds of breakdown to deal with: minor mechanical, major mechanical, and electrical. Some of each category can be fixed and some can't. Of the three, the electrical problems most often stop the nomad. They are in essence the easiest of repairs, since they usually involve nothing more than replacing a wire or connection or a fuse. But they are the hardest problems for the amateur to diagnose and will often elude even the most diligent search.

Your mount runs on air, gasoline, oil, and electricity. Beyond broken or disconnected mechanical parts, most breakdowns occur because of a flow interruption in one or more of those systems. All repair and analysis procedures are designed to trace these flow systems from beginning to end, checking for interruptions. You have run your dunce's checks — key on, gas in the tank, plugs attached, etc. — and have isolated your problem a little by considering the points in Procedure Three. Given this starting point, you know which of the four systems to approach first: oil, gas, air, or electricity.

Here are the procedures for checking each system, starting with the simplest (gas) and saving the electrics for last.

"Oh, look, honey! There's no gas in the tank."

Procedure Four: Check Gas Flow

Gasoline runs from the fuel tank through a line or lines into the carburetor(s) and thus into the cylinders of your engine. If the flow is blocked anywhere along this passage, your engine will quit.

Start at the top. Look in the tank. You've got gas?

Pull the fuel line off the bottom of the tank. There will be a petcock there. Open it momentarily. Gas? If not, take your tank off, turn it on its side, and pull the petcock. Clean it and the dirt trap attached to it, which fits inside your gas tank. Get out your cook kit and fill your pots with gasoline while you rinse out the inside of your tank with more gas.

If the petcock was clean, blow out your fuel line and reconnect the whole thing. Move to the carburetor. You have a tickle valve on it. Depress this until the float bowl floods. If it won't flood, your carburetor's blocked.

Pull the carb and dismantle it, being very careful not to lose parts and such. Pull the drain plug first and watch for dirt or water. Check the needle valve and float assembly. Blow out all those little orifices in the carb; dirt in any of them will stop your engine. Check to see that the valve moves freely when you work the throttle, so that the float isn't sticking either open or closed.

If fuel is getting into and through your carbs, check to see that your engine valves aren't sticking. If they are working freely, you are definitely getting gasoline to the business section and your problem is not in the gas flow.

Procedure Five: Check Air Flow

Air enters your mount through an air filter or cleaner, is then sucked into the carburetor, mixed with fuel, and blown into the cylinder. Without air — or, more properly, oxygen — the engine will not fire.

Start your air-flow procedure at the air cleaner. Most modern bikes have a paper filter system, which sucks incoming air through a porous fiber mat that keeps dust and dirt out. If this mat is clogged it cannot breathe and neither can your engine. Take the filter out and clean it by either banging it gently on the ground or blowing through it from the back. If your bike has one of the old "oil" air filter systems, or something weird (Ganesh has a steel-wool filter!), clean it according to the instructions in your manual. Oil-type air filters can be filled with engine oil, in a pinch. In a real emergency you can leave the cleaner off and ride without one, but that's inviting an engine rebuild if you happen to suck a few rocks into the engine.

Check the flange on the carburetor. Is it tight? A loose carburetor top means air leakage, which means hard starts and poor running — and may be the reason you're sitting by the road.

Check the carb intake to see that your slide is working. If you can't see into it, stick your finger in and work the throttle with the other hand. The slide controls the throat opening into the carb and thus the amount of air. Checking the slide this way will tell you if the throttle cable has broken — something you often cannot tell just by twisting the grip.

When reinstalling the carb be *very* gentle. Tighten the flange down with care, evenly and smoothly. If you warp the flange, or the carb itself, you will have destroyed the only throat your mount has, and it will fall over dead.

If you have air into and through the carb, and it isn't leaking away at the flange or the gaskets, then your problem is not in the air-flow system unless it rests in adjustments, which are covered separately under Procedure Eight.

Procedure Six: Check Oil Flow

Oil lubricates your engine, covering all the moving parts with a film that staves off friction. In four-stroke engines it is a separate system, and in two-strokers it is incorporated into the gasoline-flow system. Oil flow will stop your machine only when there is too little of it available. In both two- and four-strokers, lack of lubrication oil will bring the bike to a screeching halt, and in two-bangers it will cause seizure.

The upper works — piston, cylinder, etc., on a two-stroker are lubricated by flinging oil into the firing chamber along with the gas and air. This is why two-burners smoke, and why they use more oil than four-posters, and why they seize when deprived.

In any bike, if you suspect oil as the villain, let the machine sit for a minimum of five minutes (which is about the time it will take you to run Procedure Two), then pull the crankcase dipstick. On your two-banger, check your automatic oil-feed mechanism. If your bike is mature enough to have been around before these devices make sure there is a little oil in the gas. (You can tell by feel.)

A seized two-banger can be made to run again by letting it cool and then adding crankcase oil to the gas tank (if your oil feed is broken) or to the oil tank (if you've simply run out). A better policy, though, is to carry enough new oil to get you home in an emergency — usually a quart will do.

You can tell a lot of things from the condition of your oil — mostly about mechanical problems. But what you're checking for now is whether you have enough. If not, and if you're carrying none, get out the tow rope. You *cannot* run your mount without oil and there is nothing you can use as a substitute.

Procedure Seven: Check Electricity Flow

If your mount is getting air, oil, and gas in all the right places, and if nothing sounds broken inside, you must look to your electrical system.

Electrics is an arcane subject to many people and a difficult one even to those who understand it. The problem for the bike nomad is made more difficult yet by the fact that there are three separate types of electric-flow systems in use by motorcycle manufacturers, by the fact that diagnosis of electrical problems is a chancy process without a lot of expensive and nonportable equipment, and by the fact that a number of common electrical emergencies just aren't repairable beside the road.

Despite all this, it is possible to get yourself moving again after an electrical breakdown if you are lucky, if you understand the basics of bike electrics, and if your break is a fixable one.

Here is a bare-bones explanation of your mount's shockworks.

How electricity works. Electricity can be regarded as a fluid. It flows from point to point along a metal path — usually a wire — isolated from other metal by insulation — usually plastic or rubber. Two things are necessary for electricity to do work: that its "flow" be uninterrupted and that the flow be circular, forming a circuit. Switches, fuses, and breaker points are ways of opening or interrupting a circuit and closing it on command. A switch is a device that *you* control. A breaker point is an automatic switch operating more precisely than your hand could. A fuse is an overload switch that interrupts the flow before it can melt the channel (the wire).

Work is performed by placing the desired object in the path of the electric flow. That is, in the circuit. Your headlight is on a circuit with a switch. When the switch is off, the circuit is interrupted and there is no flow. When the switch is on, the flow moves across the switch gap and on to your headlight, heating the filament — producing the "work" — and then moves on around the circuit back to the generating equipment. By having many circuits and many switches, the electric flow on your mount can be made to do several kinds of work independent of other work. You can run your lights without having your horn on all the time, and run the bike without your lights, and so forth.

All electrical ills on your bike are some form of electric-flow interruption or overload. When diagnosing an electrical problem, follow this procedure:

Flow interruptions should be checked first: chafed or broken wire, blown fuses, open switches, visible shorts. Start with the fuses because they are the most visible and easily corrected problem. If they are okay, look over your wiring harness carefully, checking for that broken wire, that worn-through spot of insulation, that jarred-loose bullet connection. Make sure your ignition switch hasn't simply vibrated to the off position. (It happens, believe me.) Are the plug leads in the plugs? Are both wires connected at the battery? These "physical" flow interruptions account for nearly all the unexpected stops your electric system makes, so no matter how dumb it feels to get off and wiggle your switches, do it.

Mechanical interruptions are next: plugs, points, battery. Start with the plugs. You've already looked to see that the high-tension lead is in place — at both ends. Now check to see if there is any electricity going through it. Pull the plug, reconnect it to the lead, and ground it against an engine fin. Kick the engine over. Do you have a spark? If not, you're in for an electrical check, which we'll get to later.

The next mechanical check is the points. They should be clean, free of oil and dirt, and have a gap about equal to the thickness of a business card. Your manual will give you the exact gap and your feeler gauge will set it for you. The points should spark when you rotate the engine (this is with the ignition switch on, of course). If not, another electrical check is in order.

Ground your battery with a tool to see if it has any juice. Look to see that there are no obvious cracks in the cells, that the water level is correct, and that the lead connections haven't corroded off.

If all of these things check out as functional, you are left to conclude that the problem is (a) electric in nature, (b) hidden from casual inspection, (c) both of the above.

Electrical interruptions are last: coil, condenser, generator, rectifier, magneto, diode. The sequence for analyzing electrical interruptions varies according to which of the three systems your mount uses. These systems are: battery ignition, magneto ignition, and CDI ignition.

Battery systems run their circuits off a battery, which is kept charged with a generator and alternator. Most four-stroke bikes use this system. The advantage is that it allows you to draw current from the battery for any of your mount's functions, even though the engine isn't running. The disadvantage is that it is a complicated system with a lot of parts that can go bad.

Magneto systems produce current only when the engine is running. This system requires fewer parts and is often more reliable, but it has a few disadvantages — besides not giving you any juice unless the power plant is turning over. Magneto systems generate current in proportion to the speed of the engine, depending on the battery (for the light circuit) to dampen current surges so as to avoid blowing your light bulbs. This in turn requires a rectifier to make direct current of the magneto's AC output, which means another part to go bad. It also requires that you be fanatic about keeping the water level up in your battery, since a dry battery will not dampen surge very much.

Most two-stroke bikes and a few four-strokers use the magneto system. The British bikes use a variation that employs a zener diode in a heat sink to bleed off excess current. When one of these things burns out, it shorts out the entire system.

The basic problem with magneto systems is that they

are intrinsically hard to work on without specialized equipment. For example, you must have current somewhere in order to test electric flow. On a battery system, the battery supplies that current. On a magneto-rigged bike, you must pack a battery along if you anticipate breaking down electrically out on the highway. Most Japanese bikes that use the magneto system build the points and other electrical parts into or inside the flywheel assembly, which makes them completely inaccessible to the nomad who doesn't happen to have the special flywheel puller the factory won't sell him anyway.

Then there is the Kawasaki CDI system, which uses no points, an exotic gapless plug, and a multitude of rarefied techniques, and which simply cannot be worked on by the amateur and cannot be tested beside the road.

In short, you stand some chance of fixing a battery system, less chance of fixing a magneto system, and no chance of fixing a CDI system.

With this in mind, get out your test light, your wiring diagram, and your spare ration of patience. You are going to trace each circuit from the battery to the end point — switch, light, etc., the idea being to isolate whatever portion of your wire isn't producing current, then to bridge over it. If your trouble is not in a replaceable device (points, plugs, condenser, etc.), this is all you can do.

If you find a dead section of wire, you can make it functional by wiring past it with some of your spare electrical wire, your test lamp with the lamp taken off and the wires twisted together, or in a real emergency, with bare wire from your tool kit.

Note: test lamps for both battery and magneto systems can be made from your flashlight, with the flashlight itself supplying the power on a magneto system. Emergency fuses can be made from tinfoil, the inner wrapper off a stick of gum, or the inner wrapper off a pack of cigarettes.

Procedure Eight: Adjustments

It isn't often that an adjustment problem will be so severe that it stops your mount, but it does happen, and in all sorts of bizarre ways. I have had the top of my port carb come off while running down the road and blow enough gasoline over the rear end to cut the grease right out of the axle and freeze the wheel!

Any badly adjusted part can be damaging. Loose rocker arms can eventually throw a rod right through your engine. A too-hot plug on your two-banger can eventually crack or hole your piston. Improperly adjusted oil-metering systems will burn the whole engine up.

The best procedure to run if your gas, oil, electricity, and air all function, and if there are no obvious problems, is to take out your owner's manual and go through all the routine maintenance and adjustment operations. Set your tappets, your timing, your plug gaps, etc.

In this "adjustments" group I will include the real disasters — broken parts. There are two or three ways to tell if your mount's illness is the result of a broken part. First, it may be visible, as when you break a chain and it wraps itself around your leg. Second, it may be audible, as when you throw that rod through the top of your cylinder. Third, it may be something you can test for, as in a holed piston. (You check that by pulling the plug and sticking your finger over the hole while you crank the engine. There should be enough compression to pop your finger off the hole smartly.)

Few internal breaks can be repaired on the road. This is because there are no extraneous parts in an engine or a transmission. If it's in there, it has a job to do. Naturally, if a part breaks, there's a job not being done, and that usually stops you.

There are exceptions. A cylinder out of commission on

a single or a twin is usually fatal to your day's plans. But on a triple or a four-cylinder, you can sometimes limp quite a long way on half your bangers. A ruined gear can be crippling, but sometimes you can chug down the road on one or two gears alone.

Basically, though, a major mechanical breakdown is cause to get out the tow rope. While you're at it, get out that fluorescent HELP! sign you have in your medicine chest. It'll get you a tow a lot faster than waving your arms.

Procedure Nine: Minor Mechanical

A minor mechanical breakdown is any break that you can see or feel, and which you can fix with wit and bailing wire. Here are a couple of common ones and their cures.

Broken cables can be replaced if you've brought your spares along. If not, run a piece of your utility wire through the cable housing. It will last long enough to get you to help. I have seen *string* used as cable successfully. Remember: a cable is a long-distance on/off switch. Anything that will give you variable throttle, clutch release, or whatever is needed is in effect a cable, even if it is a stick.

Broken levers can be faked several ways. Handlebar levers can be made by taping one side of a pair of pliers to the bars, then taping or clamping the cable to the other side. Clamp with those plumbers' clamps you've got in your toolbox.

Foot levers can be made by clamping your vise grips to the shaft where the lever went. This destroys the splines, but it will get you down the road. You can also use your vise grips for footpegs, axle nuts, and any other external break that requires nothing except a quick stop to fix.

Lost nuts or bolts can often be overlooked if they are

one of a series — as the side case screws, for example. If the missing bolt or nut is vital in itself, or if its lack will cause you to leak oil or something, you can cure it several ways, some more drastic than others.

You can fake a nut by winding some of your wire around the bolt. This will hold if it's done right, and hold well. For a nut that takes heavy strain, and which you cannot clamp your vise grips over, haul out your plumbers' hose clamps again. I once held the swing-arm axle of a Puch in place this way for 600 miles.

As a last resort, a glob of your liquid aluminum will work perfectly as a surrogate nut. But when you get home, you'll have to saw the bolt off.

You can fake a bolt with any material that will fill the hole, provided the strain on the bolt won't break the material. I've seen everything from rolled-up cardboard to wire-wrapped pencils used in place of screws and bolts when the occasion was desperate enough.

Best bet, if you really have to get down the highway, is to take a smaller bolt, a core of wrapped wire, or any similar thing with strength, coat it with liquid aluminum, and plug the hole with it.

If you are astoundingly patient and lucky, you can *make* a bolt by casting one of the size you need in clay, cutting the mold carefully with your knife, and filling it with the plastic metal. I have never tried this but I know of three nomads who swear to have either done it or seen it done, and it sounds like it would work!

Ultimately, then, your best armor against roadside breakdowns is preparation. This preparation includes having the right tools and spare parts, the right attitudes, and a thorough knowledge of the mechanical and electrical functions of your mount.

Part of your attitude must be the knowledge that sometime, somewhere, you are going to sputter to a halt, and you must be capable of approaching the moment with humor and patience. These two attitudes are the universal tools, and without them you will find yourself doing three times the necessary work, or doing things over again.

When there is no longer any hope of repairing your mount and you must seek outside help, do so with flair. Be the sort of person that passersby want to stop and help.

And part of that is being the sort of person who stops to help others.

Wisdom

"Trouble seeks all but most often finds the unprepared."

"Alertness to trouble is the best defense against it."

16.
The Oasis

To this point we have dealt with the founding of your mobile home, with putting it on wheels, and with the techniques of moving it along the road. In this last part of the Highways Section, we'll treat the most common aspect of two-wheel nomadics: staying still.

On the average, you will spend less than four hours a day in the saddle. The rest of the time will be spent stationary. If this seems a low riding average, consider that most nomads ride eight hours a day — when they ride; they camp a couple of days every three or four days. In real time, this means that five-sixths of your living will be done off your mount. It therefore behooves us to give some thought to all that open time.

To that end, we will divide your "stopping" time into that which you spend in the country and that which you spend in the city.

This chapter and the next one deal with the "country" portions. And we start with the right-turn signal you give as you pull off the freeway in the warm dusk, following the sign to the oasis.

Parks and Campgrounds

We have today a unique concept in nomadics, the commercial oasis. In the historic sense all oases have been commercial. But they became towns and cities, places in which to escape the rigors of the wilderness.

Now we have oases in the wilderness, designed to help us escape the rigors of the city. The problem with most of these new oases — campgrounds — is that they bring much of the city into the wilderness with them, to the general detriment of the environment and the participants.

Parks and campgrounds have their advantages for the nomad, though, and there are times when nothing else will quite do. I'd like to look for a moment at the kinds, number, and location of parks.

"Park" and "campground" are used here to mean any place specifically designed or designated for the use of overnight campers. These fall into one of three categories: national grounds, state and municipal grounds, and privately owned grounds. In each group there are free camps, cheap camps, expensive camps, and outright rip-offs. In each group there are paradises and cesspools, and you cannot always go by type, location, name, or cost. You cannot even go on another nomad's word, since his idea of Eden may not always be yours. Nor are camps always homogenous things. A man who camps in the swampy bottom of a lakeside park is not going to get the same view of the park as the man who camps on top of the hill, especially if it rains.

National campgrounds comprise the smallest group, but the best known and most widely used. The reason for this is simple: the government owns the majority of the scenic land in the United States. Although national campgrounds comprise the smallest group, they include some of the biggest individual campgrounds, places like Yosemite, with 760,900 acres, or Colorado's Routt National Forest, with 1,125,000 acres, or Arizona's Grand Canyon area, with 673,000 acres.

The prime advantage of a national park is the National Park Service ranger, who is to park wardens what the Texas Rangers were to frontier lawmen. National Park Service men are the best trained, best behaved and most conscientious environmentalists around, and any park they run will be run as nearly right as local conditions permit. They are to a remarkable degree free of politics and power. So much so that the bad national park ranger is the exception rather than the rule.

The benefits of this, for the two-wheel nomad, are found in the conditions under which he makes his stay. A clean, well-managed campground and a friendly ranger can make a lot of difference in the way you get up in the morning.

Another advantage of the national park is that it often costs less than a comparable commercial or state-owned park. Many national campgrounds honor the Golden Eagle pass, which is a thing you buy from the government for $7 (as of 1973) and which gets you free admission or reduced rates at national campgrounds. Even without a pass, the national campground usually costs under $2 a night, with reduced rates if the site is taken by the week or longer.

The last advantage of the national campground is that above-mentioned penchant the government has for owning the really scenic spots. The advantage lies not so much in the scenery as in the fact that grandeur is usually located a long way from the pollution centers, so the air, water, and vibrations are purer — even when filled with weekend city persons.

State and municipal campgrounds are the largest group, numerically speaking. They are, conversely, often the smallest parks, running from an average of 100 acres in the state parks to less than 3 acres in the municipal parks.

The advantages of state parks lie in their accessibility

and numbers. You are never too far from a state park with camping facilities, no matter where yóu are. Most are seasonal, though, and the farther north you get the shorter the season.

The disadvantage of state parks is that they are erratic in quality. Some will be maintained well but overused, with a net result totaling poor camping. Some will be virtually use-free but also nearly free of maintenance, with the same result as above.

I have found that, on the whole, the condition of a state's public parks depends on the state itself. There are some states that welcome the tourer with open arms, and others that welcome him with open cash registers. In general, though, the farther south you are, the better the state camps tend to be, with the state of Texas shining brightly above all others.

Municipal campgrounds are usually free or very cheap. They are also likely to be dirty and full of midnight beer-can tossers. The rule on municipal campgrounds is: give yourself time to get to another campground when you look at a municipal park.

The real problem with city parks is that they are almost never listed in anything but city brochures. They are too small and too numerous to be carried in the big campground atlases and are mostly considered as competition by the state campgrounds, so aren't listed in their guides, either. This leaves you to seek them out usually sight unseen and with no prior feedback.

Privately owned grounds will soon be the largest numerical group due to the fact that one person can buy a piece of land and turn it into a campground about fifty times faster than a city, a state, or the Great White Fathers can. The reason this is being done is that, as I noted at the start of this book, there are almost more people on the road than at home today.

Generally speaking, the privately owned campground is to the wilderness what Howard Johnson's is to the home. In fact, most private campgrounds — especially the chains — are not much different than your own house. They have Laundromats, grocery stores, movie houses, swimming pools, television sets, etc. The only difference is that in your own house you don't have to pay $4.50 a night for the privilege of sleeping on the ground.

Commercial campgrounds often have good locations (as opposed to scenic ones). They will be strategically near some natural or man-made attraction. They are the most expensive group of grounds, and the very worst that campgrounds can become will be found in this category.

The salient characteristic of the above is that it is all subject to exception. There are great campgrounds in the north; there are exquisite privately owned camps; there are national parks where the grocery store gets $1.35 for a dozen eggs; city parks where you could eat off the ground.

On the whole, the best camps are those that are least used or least known and that have managements sympathetic to the park and its users. Many of these could easily handle ten times the flow they are getting without damage to the environment or the psyche. In the Sources Appendix I have included a small list of campgrounds that I have found to be exceptional in some way.

When to Stay in a Campground

The real reason there are so many campgrounds is that there are so few other places where you can camp, particularly if you are staying longer than overnight. This has become a country of fences, and fences are anathema to the nomad.

You stay in a campground when you need the company

of fellowmen, when you need the services offered by civilization, and when you need assurance that someone won't roust you out in the middle of the night to throw you off his land.

The company of your peers can get to be a problem if you aren't lucky. This is especially so in the more crowded campgrounds. Pets will carry your supper off, kids will carry your gear off, and sometimes people will carry you off. A friend of mine was bedded down among the pickup campers in a popular chain campground. He got up to answer nature's insistent call and while he was doing so one of the truckers fired up his rig and drove out — right over my friend's tent.

This sort of thing is more the rule than the exception in the big, overcrowded campgrounds. I could recite dozens of similar stories.

Campgrounds offer the only campsites you can usually find within walking distance of urban services. You can eat or do laundry or anything else in the city, but you must do so while tending your mount and watching the local sticky-fingers. It is sometimes nice to be able to throw your laundry in the machine while you cook dinner a few yards away, knowing that you don't have to repack your entire home as soon as the clothes are dry. The trick lies in finding a campground that gives you a sensible number of services without becoming so urbanized that it is an extension of Main Street.

The rule is: the longer you will be in camp, the farther away your urban services can be. If you're just off the road for the night, you won't want to drive 6 miles into town merely to buy some beans. But if you're in camp for a week or so, a nice shopping drive will feel good.

The best advantage of formal campgrounds is that you can show up at midnight, bleary-eyed and exhausted, throw the fee at the attendant, and pitch your bedroll,

knowing that you'll be allowed to sleep as long as you want. This is part of the overall concept of protection that an organized operation has. In a campground, you are endangered only by the thoughtlessness of your fellow campers, and help is near at hand. In the wild, or on somebody's land, you are often considered fair game for everything from indignant rousting to being potshotted.

Stay in campgrounds when (a) you are unfamiliar with the area, (b) you are making time and haven't the hours necessary to hunt up a free camp, (c) you know a given ground to be a good place to stop, (d) you are tired.

When to Avoid Campgrounds

And whenever you can, avoid the formal campground! Do this because the "found" camp is more fun, because it is usually free, because it will teach you more about yourself and your world, and because each time you find a new one you are adding it to a personal atlas that will one day make you invisible — which is a nomadic trait. (More on this later.)

You can pass up the campgrounds when you know the surrounding countryside well enough to find a personal camp, when you have sufficient time to scout one up — and go to a formal campground if you fail in your search — when you are in an area bereft of campgrounds, and when you simply want to be alone with the world you're passing through.

All of which is predicated on your knowing what constitutes a potential free camp and on your ability to recognize and use it.

The Invisible Man

There is not one acre of "free" land in the continental United States. Every inch of this country's soil is owned by a person, company, or government. Those parcels of land not directly deeded to some party are blanket-deeded to a municipal, state, or federal government.

In theory, this means that there are no places you can legally camp on except land you own yourself, land you have written permission to use, and those designated campgrounds I've been urging you to avoid. In practice, this situation can be bettered considerably, since most of the land in America lies unused, unwanted, or uncared for. A great deal of this land is available to the motorcycle nomad if he is sensible in choosing his site, if he maintains certain attitudes about the land and his place on it, and if he has a healthy respect for the potency of the printed word in official form. Knowledge of how much more valuable property is than people in this society leads to respect for the printed word, and that respect, combined with a proper attitude toward the land, will guide you to a sensible choice of site.

Finding free campsities is an art, much like effortless

riding. It comes of practice and surviving your mistakes. It can, however, be reduced to words and systems like any other art. The "art" is in the proficiency and grace with which you practice your skills.

The point around which all this revolves is invisibility, the nomad's ability to come, stay, and go without making his presence known more than is necessary and without leaving a mark behind him. This is one of the oldest of the nomad's arts, and the chiefest of his skills, save only his riding ability.

The practice of being invisible has three parts: coming, staying, and going.

Coming means selecting your site for invisibility. Invisibility can mean actual camouflage, having permission to use a site, removal from traffic, etc. Anything, in other words, that lowers the odds on your being hassled for using a site. The best of these is having permission to use the land. After this comes removal from traffic. A piece of desert is less likely to draw attention to you than a roadside camp. Worst is having such a site that you must rely on actual concealment to avoid being approached.

Staying means living on your site so that you displace as little nature as possible and damage nothing. This means that it's okay to wash in a stream, but don't do your laundry in it. Use driftwood or standing deadwood and don't cut trees. If you dig a latrine or a drainage ditch, save the sod and cover it over when you leave.

Going means being able to look back at your camp and not being able to tell you've been there.

Of these three kinds of invisibility, the first is the most important. You can learn quite easily how to run a clean and invisible camp because there are a thousand books on the subject. But there are no texts on how to assess a given site's invisibility.

Here is a three-vector system for doing just that. The

factors involved are: length of stay, location, ownership. Each factor must be considered independently, then vectored with the remaining two before you can determine your site's suitability.

Staying time, the first factor, means how long you will be stopping. The importance of this lies in the degree of sophistication your camp must have. If you're just going to catch a nap, you can pull over and sleep on the grass. If you're staying overnight, you have to unpack your bag and maybe your tent. If you're staying a week, you'll need that latrine, a food-supply source nearby, washing facilities, etc. You must therefore consider the time element when choosing your site because it determines the *size* of your camp or, if you prefer, the degree to which you will impinge on your environment.

Location is obvious. You will have to think of what your camp will look like from the air, from highways, from farmhouses, etc. This is often a tricky prospect. I once found a peaceful wood a mile off the road, with a little stream, few insects, and lots of silence. It was unfenced land that showed no sign of cultivation, was posted against hunting (though not against trespass), and bore no mark of recent or regular use. I made a nice, two- or three-day camp and went to sleep. The next morning I got run over by about forty motorcycles. Seemed that my woods were in the center of a local cowtrailing club's grounds!

Roughly, these first two factors interdepend thus: the shorter your stay, the less invisible you have to be. However, the precise opposite can hold true, depending on the final factor, ownership.

Ownership has two aspects for the would-be invisible nomad: who owns the land and how close is he? Certain kinds of owner are easy to deal with because they are at hand, such as the farmer, whom you can ask for permission to camp in his field, and the local game warden, who can tell you where some good bets for campsites are. Others are easy to deal with because of their absence, such as the federal government, which might or might not ask you to leave a piece of its land if it were there to see you, but it isn't.

When vectoring these three factors, strive *first* for ownership qualification, then for location, then for length of stay. The prime question you must ask yourself when choosing a free camp is: what will the likely consequences be if I am asked to leave? The rule is: if your site is owned by a person, the chances are that you can make an amicable arrangement; if it's owned by a company, you can sometimes make an arrangement; if it's owned by a government, you can seldom make an arrangement. But then, the government-owned land is most often free of observers, so the scale runs exactly backwards on this point!

Vector your probable staying time against both the visibility of your site and the likelihood of an owner's coming to throw you off. Try for permission first.

Finally, we get to the "where to camp" part. Here are a number of places I've found as campsites, classified according to the vector system above.

Short Camps: High Visibility

Areas on federal highway rights of way. This means the center strips on the interstate system highways, the cloverleaf areas (which often have grassy patches around them), the grassy areas around the off/on ramps. Useful only in emergencies because of high visibility and the certainty of a visit from the highway patrol. I have camped twice on cloverleaf areas when I was too tired to ride on, waiting until the state patrol stopped and explaining my situation before bedding down, and once in a lightly wooded center strip with Ganesh camouflaged and no tent up, explaining nothing and stealing away at first light.

Abandoned farms and buildings. These offer some wind and rain shelter, depending on their state of preservation, but tend to attract tourists, lovers, strange people, and the occasional ax murderer. They also harbor insect and rodent life of great ferocity, and many times are dangerous in themselves due to disrepair.

Short Camps: Low Visibility

Areas near but not actually in campgrounds. There is usually an amount of woods, mountain, field, etc., surrounding a campground, and you can quite often lie up for a night quite peacefully, especially since one more nomad won't be that noticeable cruising around a campground.

Rights of way and adjacent areas off farm roads. These roads, used almost exclusively by local traffic, nearly always have a couple of thickets per mile that will shelter a bike nomad nicely for a night or two. The trick is to find one that doesn't appear to do regular service as a trysting spot.

The areas behind large truck stops. Not on the tarmac, necessarily, but off behind the used-tire dumps. The advantage here, of course, is in the nearness of facilities. This is a particularly good bet in the West, where the huge truckers' villages are built out in the desert with a lot of nothing around them — all yours for camping on.

Long Camps: High Visibility

You can throw up camp for a considerable length of time in the open desert, the middle of a cornfield (not on the corn), on the sides of hills, and on small islands in the middle of streams. All these sites are visible to anyone who looks, but some will be in positions where no one looks and others in positions where no one bothers if they do see you. Likewise, the cany bottom of a river that runs along a highway will often provide you with a campsite, especially if you choose it to minimize casual spotting.

The secret of the high-visibility camp is traffic patterns. You must choose your camp so as to avoid the passing flow, remembering that being invisible is accomplished mostly by staying out of the line of sight of your fellow citizens. Niño Cochise became invisible to the U.S. government during the Indian pogroms by being erased from the rolls. He existed in the flesh as a small boy, but as far as the government was concerned, he was invisible. When he later moved into the mountain fastness Geronimo set up for his war with the Mexicans and the Americans, he was invisible in fact. But *each form* of invisibility had been effective!

Long Camps: Low Visibility

The ultimate free camp is one where you have access to the facilities you need and freedom from hassle, and have this for as long as you want it. You can find such camps in a number of places. There are many, many abandoned buildings, farms, factories, and even whole towns that are well off the beaten path and that can offer the nomad shelter. They have the same hazards as their near-the-highway cousins but are much less visible. You can often find these places by asking at local gas or food stops, prominently displaying your camera and expressing interest in the scenic beauties of abandoned buildings.

As a rule, the farther into the wilderness you get, the more permanently you can erect a camp without being bothered by other people. And there is still a staggering amount of wilderness left in America. Most of it is more accessible to the biker than to anyone else, because his mount will get into places where a jeep won't, and it will carry him farther than a hiker can get. I have taken Ganesh a day's ride back into the central California mountains and been in places that have yet to feel the print of a human foot. The nearest humans were the passengers in the PSA jets overhead, and everyone else was miles and miles off.

The rule for getting into the wilderness is: move at right angles to the trails that men leave. If there is a road heading northeast, go southeast or northwest. Men don't build trails for pleasure, only for profit. And where man's roads go, so goes man.

All of the above deals with where to stay if you cannot find an owner or other responsible person whose permission you can secure. While this situation is not really desirable, it is common enough that I've included it. It is far, far better to make arrangements with someone than to depend on his goodwill should he discover you camped uninvited.

The Gypsy Secret

The great adventure is meeting other people. This is the single most hazardous, exciting, and rewarding experience of the human condition, and nothing lends itself to meeting people so readily as nomadics.

When seeking permission to use enough of a person's property to camp on, think of yourself as a Gypsy. These nomads have survived the centuries with no permanent home, dependent always on the goodwill of the citizens around them — and this with an unsavory reputation to contend with. That they have done well at survival is due in large part to what I call the Gypsy Secret, which is . . . perfect honesty.

When you deal with someone, state your needs simply and directly. If you're looking for a place to camp for a week, don't tell the person you'll be there only overnight. If you need the use of a bathroom, or of his pond, or of his barn, say so. Don't give the impression that you are a self-contained unit if you aren't.

Conversely, point out that you are a professional camper, that you will respect his property and leave it in the same condition you found it in, and that you will not interfere with the routine of his life.

I have found that with a little experience you can judge whether or not a person will allow you the use of his property almost without asking. I have also found that an offer of labor on my part goes a long way toward making my presence acceptable to the person.

In sum, the oasis is anywhere the nomad can find it. He will sometimes have to pay to rest his head, sometimes not, and sometimes he must fold his tent and steal away in the dawn.

17.
Reading the Sign

The two-wheel nomad, like the sailor and the pilot, must be adept at reading the language of weather and of the road. He must also be familiar with the various maps that other men have made to make his passage easier.

The purpose of maps is to provide aid, usually directional. That is, a map is not "help" in itself, but a method of finding help. In this last chapter in the Highways Section, we will consider the kinds of aid a biker looks for, and the maps he or she uses for each. We begin with road maps.

Maps and What Kind to Get

In most European and Asian countries you have to buy road maps. In the United States we take them for granted because they are free. This is unfortunate because anything taken for granted will invariably be ill-used. Most of us have no idea of the wealth of information that can be found on a road map or inferred from it. We regard a map primarily as a device for choosing routes and figuring mileages.

Yet, by careful perusal and some thought you can use a state or regional road map to figure the likelihood of shelter in a given area, the nearest services of the type you need, the campgrounds you can reach, the scenic routes available to you, the quickest route through urban areas, and even the odds on running into bad weather!

For example, you are in Memphis in the afternoon, taking a break before heading west. Little Rock, Arkansas, is about 140 miles away, and that's where you'll be when night falls. You look at your map.

Expressway all the way. Three hours travel time. One gas stop. There's a bayou — Two Prairie Bayou — crossing the road near Lonoke. Possible camp, definite resting spot.

National forest just past Hot Springs. Another hour's ride but much better camping facilities. Dirt roads and fire breaks up around Ouachita Lake, which argues well for finding a low-visibility camp somewhere up in the woods. Mountains in the park. Elevation means cold nights, possible fog. A lot of designated campgrounds, so there will be a grocery and a Laundromat somewhere near.

The free road maps you get in gas stations are accurate and versatile, but they are updated only about every three years. This means that they seldom show current construction, and cannot show construction completed after the map was published. This often leaves you pondering whether that section of freeway marked "scheduled for completion in 1974" has been or not.

An atlas-type road map, with sectional maps laid out in book form, is good to have if you are seeking local directions and if you have the current issue. But atlases are hard to read for cumulative distance and cannot, of course, be read visually for long-distance estimation. They are also expensive and must be bought fresh each year to be effective.

An atlas, is, however, the most convenient packaging of road maps I've seen yet.

The final alternative in road maps is the auto club "map service" map. These are trip maps supplied by the various auto clubs that are marked with the latest and most accurate information on road conditions, construction, hazards, and points of interest. The value of these maps is obvious, the drawback only that you must obtain one for each routing you make — which means you must have a preplanned itinerary. There is also the fact that some clubs charge for this service, which can get expensive. I have never utilized an auto-club map service but the general consensus among nomads is that the AAA has the best.

The rule on road maps is: get a single brand. Most free maps offered by gas stations are manufactured by one company per brand. Follow this policy of consistency because each map maker uses slightly different markings and registers slightly different services. If you learn to read the Rand McNally maps that Gulf carries, for example, you'll read local roads as solid or parallel blue lines. But on Chevron's Gousha Company maps, local roads are registered as black or gray. A marking that means "historical cemetery" on one make of map means "tourist services" on another.

The other reason for using one brand of map is that if you choose the brand carried by your favorite gasoline dealer it will often show the location of service stations carrying your favorite gas, which is a good thing to know when you're low on both gas and money and it's two in the cold, cold morning.

Campground Directories

Aside from your road maps, you will need another kind of map, a campground directory. A campground atlas is a book of maps designed to locate, describe, and direct you toward campgrounds. You have two reasons for getting one of these: to help you locate campgrounds, naturally, and to complete your road-map system.

The requirements of a campground atlas are as follows:

That it carry a complete list of campgrounds.

That it give you some idea of the facilities and costs at each.

That it offer clear directions to these camps.

That its information be reliable.

Any atlas that cannot meet *all* those requirements need not be considered. A good one will carry all this and more.

There are many campground atlases on the market, but only one I would consider owning. It is the *Campground Atlas of the United States and Canada,* put out by Kalmbach Publishing Company, Milwaukee, Wisconsin 53233, and costs $4. It has a front section of maps with campgrounds spotted in and numbered, and a back section with each campground described in detail. I have found this guide to be the most consistently accurate and up-to-date atlas available.

Your campground atlas has value as a road map because it gives you local scales and thus saves you carrying regional, local, and campground maps. With the regional maps from your gas station or auto club, your campground atlas should provide all the paper guide you need, no matter how far back in the hills you wish to get.

Down and Out in Boone, Oklahoma

Sooner or later you will find yourself alone and in need of a friend in a small, remote town. For this kind of situation you need another kind of map: a personal telephone directory. This map will guide you to people who know your name and care for your safety and comfort. Your directory should contain the following numbers:

Friends, as many and as widely scattered as possible.

Try for people who will *really* pitch for you when you can't do it yourself.

Levers. This means folk of position whose name or place will carry weight. It helps if you know a governor or two, but anybody with a title will be better than no one at all.

Your mechanic, your bike dealer, and anybody else who might be of help in case your mount goes lame. Don't discard this simply because your mechanic is in Maine and you're in San Diego. He might know a reliable man where you are.

Family, if they are of any use in emergencies.

Legal aid, as in your lawyer.

Tape three dimes to the inside cover of your directory and forget them until you need them — and that means for emergencies, not for cigarettes or calling a ladyfriend.

Money, Quick and Slow

The most versatile aid around is money. When you are down and out there is nothing that will accomplish so much for you. To make sure you have it when you really need it, carry some quick money with you and leave some slow money behind. "Quick" money means travelers' checks, folded away in the bottom of your wallet and forgotten. Carry travelers' checks — and keep them folded away — because you'll have to work to spend them. You'll have to rob your emergency stash, unfold the things, sign and present them. All of which will work to discourage random or impulse spending of your last-ditch bread.

"Slow" money is that which you've left with a responsible party and which you can get to only by phone or wire. Do this in case all the above precautions have failed and you've spent your bail money on ice cream, in case you've lost your bread, been robbed, or any of the other astounding things that can part a person from his money.

The thing to remember with slow money is that the party holding it has to be reachable at all hours. I have made arrangements with my bank, which keeps constant, long hours. I am never more than a day away from my slow money, nor hours away from a confirmation that it's there — in case a local official needs reassurance.

Reading the sign includes a final aspect, local conditions. As you pass through an area, check with the people coming the other way for weather and road conditions, for hazards and shortcuts, for peculiarities in the landscape, people, or whatever. Ask policemen about local conditions, state patrolmen about conditions within a few hours' ride, and truckers about things a few hundred miles away.

The single biggest problem you'll have in reading sign is weather. You'll find that you will outride local weather forecasts and that regional ones are usually too vague to be of much help. The best you can do is stay prepared for the worst (see weatherpacking again) and hope for good weather. In the oasis, this is of little import except to your recreational life, but when riding it can be a problem.

This concludes the Highways Section, though not everything has been said about riding motorcycles, or about the oasis, or even about equipment! But we've looked at the major aspects of going and stopping for the two-wheel nomad; we've covered the vital tools and attitudes; we've looked at a few more tricks.

In the next section, Cities, we'll consider how all this applies to life in the concrete canyons.

Wisdom

"Find the stones before you lie down."
— Boy Scout Manual

"The more time you spend lookin' over yer camp, th' less time you'll spend regrettin' yer decision."
— John Rogers

PART 3: CITIES

A city is . . .

A concrete forest.
A way to keep people off the farm.
The highest point of human endeavor.
The lowest point of human endeavor.
A vector system.
A problem-solving matrix.
An excuse for highways.
The most absurd sex substitute yet devised.

18.

When in Rome

As a two-wheel nomad you will have much converse with cities. You'll pass through them, camp in them, and deal with their citizens. The chances are that you are already familiar with cities, since less than 7 percent of our population is rural today, but you'll find that urban people's reactions to you are greatly altered when you appear on a motorcycle with your home strapped aboard. You will have to learn an entirely different approach to people-contact once you've become a motorcycle tourist.

This section is concerned with showing you some of those changes and how to handle them. It also deals with nomadic problems peculiar to the cities, such as shelter, special riding techniques, money manipulation, etc. It concludes with a final chapter on the philosophy of nomadism and the Sources Appendix.

It starts with this chapter on dealing with city folk.

The Vandal Effect and How to Cure It

Throughout history there has been a basic schism between the settled people of the farm and town and the wandering people of the road and plain. The townfolk have looked upon the nomad as a plunderer and murderer at worst and a force for chaos at best. The nomad has seen the farmer and merchant as stolid and unimaginative, as robbers with pens and writs for weapons.

There has been more than a little truth in both viewpoints.

However diluted, this attitude persists today. There is an almost instinctive unease among many settled people when a motorcyclist comes on the scene, particularly if he is obviously a nomad. This unease can manifest itself in many forms but most often it shows as rudeness or hostility toward the biker. If the biker returns it, another layer is added to the myth-cake, and the batter is muddled for the next nomad to come down the road.

And yet, who can blame anyone? The tales of bikers who have ripped off gas stations, been vulgar in restaurants, and insulted women are legion, as are the tales of service stations with "NO BIKERS" signs, people who sic their dogs on motorcyclists, etc. Remember that *cave canum* — beware the dog — is as old as Pompeii; settled folk abhor intrusion, and the nomad is an intrusion.

It is your job — since you are the foreign element — to make the necessary moves to assuage the urban citizen's fears and acquire his help and respect. You do this by developing an attitude tailored to the situation and by bearing in mind some basic principles of human psychology.

Speaking Your Native Language

One of the traits common to both merchants and nomads is a facility in talking with other people, for both come in contact with strangers on a regular basis. The merchant, if he stays in business, learns an essential fact about human psychology: he'll catch more customers with respect than with sales or discounts. The successful merchant will present a friendly, respectful countenance to his potential customer no matter what he feels about that person's probable habits or lifestyle. He may dislike people with long hair, or dark skin, or Slavic names, but he'll address each as "sir" or "ma'am" and be courteous. He does this because his livelihood is more important to him than his prejudices.

The two-wheel nomad will do well to adopt this policy of giving the new acquaintance first respect. It involves no subservience, costs nothing, and will often be the difference between a hostile and a friendly reception. It can be employed anywhere, anytime, by anyone.

If the first rule for speaking your native language is courtesy and respect — which gets the other person's attention in the right way — the second rule is: speak the local dialect. This country is so vast that it contains more dialects than Europe has languages. And a knowledge of the dialect employed in the area you're visiting helps smooth your passage.

Note that I use "dialect" more in the sense of language peculiarities than in the sense of speaking quirks. The quickest way to alienate someone is to mimic his oddities of speech and convince him that you are mocking him. What I suggest here is that you learn to expect German words and phrasings in the language when you're in central Pennsylvania, Mexican turns of phrase along the Texas border, English diphthonging on the Virginia Tidewater coast, etc., and that you learn to use a few of these phrases and mannerisms correctly. This can be an adventure in itself and one of the delights of nomadism. It can also make you friends more quickly than anything I've known.

The third rule for speaking your native language is: adopt a universally acceptable image when meeting new people. To an extent we do this all the time, striving for an image that will say about us what we wish said and that will impress the maximum number of people in the way we wish to impress them.

For the bike nomad this process is one of allaying fears

in the people he or she meets. When you show up on a motorcycle you come as a direct descendant of all the grade-Z biker movies and everything the citizen has seen or read about outlaw bikers. To the average nonrider, all motorcycles look alike and all bike riders are outlaws. It is your task to adopt an image that counteracts this and to wear it like a suit wherever you go. My own garment is woven of soft, precise words spoken with a smile and a little overplaying of my natural Tennessee accent. I make no hostile moves, carry myself upright, and try to be the kind of person whom dogs and children would like. In other words, I act like the Good Guys and keep my white hat visible at all times.

In your initial contacts with city people, then, be courteous, be quiet, smile, and throw in some small localism. This takes practice only for a short time, then it becomes second nature. It works with service-station attendants, waitresses, the teller at the bank, even the guy behind the counter at a motorcycle dealer's.

There is one class of city citizen who needs special attention, though.

The Officer of the Law

There are, in addition to the above rules of behavior, a few specific things the nomad must do when dealing with the officer of the law.

In most instances your meeting with a law officer will be his idea, not yours, and initiated by a flashing light. Your approach to dealing with him starts as soon as you notice his command to pull over, and the sequence goes like this:

First, put your head in the right place. You may or may not know why you are being pulled over, but in either case, keep in mind that the man behind you (a) has a lethal weapon in his possession, (b) has some degree of permission to use it, and (c) may have had a hard day. He may be stopping you for any reason from saving your life — such as noticing that your center stand is about to fall off and jam into your rear wheel — to taking out his frustrations on the first longhair hippie freak he can reach. It happens both ways quite regularly.

Next, pull over carefully and dismount. Keep your hands in plain sight and *don't move fast!* The officer doesn't know that it's only your wallet you're pulling out of your pocket. I once reached into my waistband for my wallet — having a hole in my jeans pocket — and found myself staring down *two* exceedingly large gun barrels. Seems that a week earlier four California state patrolmen had been massacred when they stopped a car for a traffic violation.

Wait until you are asked for your license, then draw it out carefully. Open it up and present it. The object in all this caution is to avoid alarming the officer. The principle is the same as that used in dealing with any potentially deadly person or object. This is not to say that you are likely to run into that one-in-several-thousand really edgy patrolman; only that if you do and you blow it, you lose. Most law officers bend over backwards so far that it's a miracle any are left. The statistics run something like a dozen officers shot by ambush or surprise for every citizen shot by accident or nerves — and that's a ratio no other country's police can match.

Still, it behooves you to avoid being one of the statistics.

Let the officer talk. Don't ask what you've done to attract his attention; he'll tell you when he's ready. When you answer his questions, apply the general rules I gave at the start of this chapter. Put your best foot forward, softly.

If your luck is running badly and you've drawn that

officer who's looking for someone to harass, bend with it and outpoint him on karma. You simply cannot win playing the hostile game. The officer has too many points on you; he's got a gun, a uniform, and the majesty of the law to hide behind, and in that game that's equal to a royal flush and a straight razor. Think anything you want, but keep it inside. Remember that he's also human — or at least Neanderthal; that you've better things to do with your time than spend it in jail or a hospital; that maybe there is some justice and he may get run over by a truck later.

Most of all, remember all the good men you've known who wore guns and badges, and remember that they don't like this guy any more than you do, for the same reason that you don't like being spit on because people equate every motorcyclist with the two-wheel losers.

The basic rule for dealing with the officer of the law is: do it his way now and make your complaints later. If you have set up your personal directory, your emergency money, and your home contacts correctly, you'll not languish in durance vile.

None of the above applies if you've just terrorized a town, robbed a bank, or rustled the sheriff's herd. If you have done wrong, then you will be taken away.

Omar Seybbid on Necessary Friendships

The nomad is more vulnerable than a settled person because he is usually a long way from his friends and vouchers when he encounters trouble. This has a tendency to make his troubles a little heavier — arresting officers are a little rougher, hospitals a little slower with the nonresident. In many cases, countering this tendency can be vital. To do so, carry all those credentials I spoke of, including that list of "levers," people of weight. Quite often the opposing forces can be softened by signs and symbols, such as letters from governors, membership cards for the Police Benevolent Association, etc. A great caravaneer of the tenth century, Omar Seybbid, made a point of visiting and gifting every official he could reach in his travels, and of securing from each of them some kind of official approval or recommendation. When he broke a new trail with his caravan he would literally shower querulous officials with writs, letters, seals, medals, and other paraphernalia designed to show these officials beyond doubt that Omar Seybbid was a person of substance and one with friends in high places.

A minor chieftain in what is now Iran once asked Seybbid how it was that he had so many friends. Omar replied that in most businesses friends were an asset; in his, a necessity.

You will find that "necessary friendships" can be potent aids in time of trouble. Among the best of these is a personal recommendation from a churchman or religious leader, particularly one who has known you for some time. It is also wise to advise your religious friend of your nomadic plans prior to leaving and to ask his or her involvement in case of trouble. Religious persons tend to be more responsible than most other people and will work harder for you than a casual friend if you're in trouble.

Remember, when you are locked up, hurt, or otherwise incapacitated, you are dependent on the goodwill of others.

The Shortest Route to Anywhere

The most consistent dealing you'll have with city dwellers is asking directions. Where is the nearest post office? Do you know a good, inexpensive restaurant? How do you get to Fifth Street from here? How do you get back on the freeway? Can I get around this group of

buildings and still be on Forty-second Street? This sort of verbal commerce will comprise better than half the traffic you have with the inhabitants of the urban areas you visit. Here are some simple hints that will ease your passage.

Routing, or actual traffic directions, should be asked of professionals, such as police officers and cabdrivers. The ordinary citizen may or may not know how to direct you from here to there but he will invariably tell you. This is usually a sincere effort, however vague or misleading, but you can run into persons who will make up directions from pure fantasy just to seem knowledgeable. If you're in one of those cities laid out by madmen following the paths of cows — like Boston or Chattanooga — you can grow old and feeble trying to get across town on the directions of well-meaning but uninformed citizens.

Service facilities, such as Laundromats, gas stations, post offices and so on, can be found from the directions of a citizen. Be sure you ask for the *nearest* facility. This not only decreases the number of directions you'll need — thus reducing error — but increases the probability that your informant knows what he or she is talking about since people tend to know their own neighborhood better than the other side of town.

Subjectives, such as "good," "inexpensive," "close," are all open to interpretation. If you ask a man the location of the nearest inexpensive Italian restaurant, you've given him three variables to consider. What does he consider near? What does inexpensive imply to him? Is "Italian" a pizza parlor or The Forum? When dealing with subjective judgments, be sure to define your terms. Instead of the above, ask him if there is a place within ten blocks where you can get a plate of ravioli for under $2. That puts parameters on everything and eliminates a lot of areas for confusion.

Emergency facilities, like hospitals, poison control centers, fire departments, etc., are most accurately reached by picking up a phone — using one of the dimes you've taped in your personal directory — and stating your location and problem to the operator, thus: "Hello. I'm unfamiliar with the town and need a doctor (lawyer, Indian chief, etc.) quickly. I'm at the corner of Sixth and Main, where do I go?"

Do it this way because when you are in an emergency situation you will tend to be excited yourself and this will translate to the person you accost for directions. He or she will more often than not get flustered by the urgency and either misdirect you or freeze up. Telephone operators are trained to handle just this sort of thing and to do it quickly and well.

Where to Find Help in a Hurry

There are two levels of "help" in the city, the official and the personal. We've been concerned above with the official in the form of systems and their operators. What if you've no recourse to telephones or the law or such? Whom do you turn to in a strange town and how do you find them?

Generally, seek persons with the same interests as yourself — which means bikers and those involved with motorcycling. You do this because such people will understand much of your problem already, because they will speak your language, because they will have empathy for you, and because they may have had similar experiences and now own the problem-solving skill you need. It's odd that a biker will think of a dealer or another rider almost automatically when he has a problem with his mount, but will seldom ask that same fellow rider's opinion on places to sleep, where to get raingear, who to see for a toothache.

The rule is: when seeking help in a strange place, look for persons who agree with your lifestyle. You can find them by looking in the places you would frequent if you lived in the city you are in.

Passing Through?

The way you deal with city folk will depend to an extent on how long you'll be in town. The longer you plan to stay, the more deeply you will be involved with the residents of the area and thus the more care you must exhibit in those dealings. Normal courtesy will see you through a trip to the grocery if you're buying a meal to cook in the night's camp 100 miles down the road, but you need to make more of an impression on the grocer if you're planning to camp on his block for a week or month.

19. SHELTER IN THE CITY

Cities are designed to handle two kinds of people: those who live there and those who transit through. Both kinds are expected to make major investments in the economy. The resident rents or buys his shelter and furniture and pays for his portion of the urban service facilities through taxes. The transient leases his shelter and services at a higher rate to make up for the rapid turnover and to make the servitors a profit.

The motorcycle nomad — indeed, any true nomad — falls outside both these categories. He carries his home with him, provides his own utilities, and needs nothing from the city but a place to tie his tent down. Since there is neither taxability nor profit in this arrangement, the city discourages nomads as parasites. I believe this question of parasitism is open to debate since no one has as yet produced a charter from the Almighty granting him the right to build a city on a piece of this planet, or the right to regulate whoever else may use it.

Be that as it may, the fact remains that few cities offer facilities suitable for nomadics. This leaves the nomad to devise his own.

The Wily Nomad

Of the facilities required by the nomad, the most difficult to procure is shelter. Food and medical and legal help are more plentiful in the city than in the wilderness, but shelter isn't. Finding shelter is mostly a matter of learning to see and a matter of how you define the word.

Six Surprises

On the road the two-wheel nomad has his tent or near-tent for shelter and a routine for its use. In the city he must change both his routine and his idea of tents. To begin with, he must *not* use his tent.

One: no tents in the city. The reasons are that a tent will be out of place to the passing eye and will draw the curious. If you erect a tent among trees, it looks natural. If you erect one among buildings — even if you're on a vacant lot — it will be as glaring a contrast as a plow horse on a racetrack.

Two: always use a shelter. This means that you don't simply throw out a sleeping bag behind the supermarket. There are a couple of reasons for this — among which are the visibility problem, the weather, and the other usual campers' problems — but the real reason is that cities attract a lot of ugly people, some of whom get their jollies by attacking women, setting fire to drunks, and sticking sharp objects into sleeping nomads. Operate on the same precautionary principles you use in the wild: avoid confrontations with dangerous animals.

Three: shelter must be large enough for your gear and should be large enough for your mount. The reasoning is obvious. Leaving your worldly possessions strapped to your mount all night is an almost 100-percent guarantee of waking up without a home. A friend and I, after an evening's discussion on the evils of city camping, tried an experiment. We parked Ganesh and my friend's mount on a busy street in a large city on the eastern seaboard. We had our gear strapped aboard, and chained the bikes to each other. We then retreated to a restaurant across the street and observed. From 7:30 P.M. to 2:00 A.M. no less than *six* separate attempts were made to shuffle off with our gear! The would-be thieves included a gang of kids, a man in a business suit, a couple of junkies, three teen-age girls, and an off-duty cop!

Four: shelter must be part of the local environment. Same reason as in One: camouflage. If you're going to sleep in a culvert (not a good idea, by the way), make sure it's in a place that looks natural for a culvert. If you find an ideal shelter, make sure it's not so ideal that someone is going to come and take it away while you sleep.

Five: shelter is anything that will keep you out of the weather and the view of the citizenry. Both conditions must be fulfilled to rate something as a shelter. This is where your ability to see comes in — "see" as in "observe accurately."

There's an old nomadic saw used to teach children to observe, and I've found it really useful. It goes:

"My son, what color is that horse?"

"It's brown, Father. On this side."

Most people don't really observe things beyond this side or this surface. It is such an ingrained habit that stage magicians have made fortunes on it, letting the audience convince itself that because a thing looks and sounds like a wooden plank, it *is* a wooden plank. Only the magician knows that it is really a shallow box with twelve feather flowers inside.

When you learn to observe, you will be able to see that a shelter is simply a weatherproof, enclosed space that is out of the line of sight of passersby.

Six: shelter must be free of occupants for the time you intend to use it. This is a problem peculiar to city camps, since you'll be using your tent in the boondocks and are the rightful inhabitant. But as most things — including trash — are someone's property in cities, you've the problem of ownership to contend with, and on a more personal level than when dealing with the owner of a piece of land out in the countryside. Therefore, you must ask yourself not only the questions you used for your vector system in Chapter Sixteen (who owns it, how far away are they, how likely are they to chase me off) but the additional question of what sort of property you are using for shelter and how likely is the owner to be upset at your usage. For instance, if you've decided to crawl into the back of an open tractor-trailer or an open boxcar (forget it, in both cases), you must ask yourself if the truck driver or railroad company is going to use this vehicle soon, and if they are likely to fling you into jail if they catch you. (The answer is yes in both those instances.)

Shelter in the city, then, is anything that will keep you out of the rain and out of the way of the citizens. It needs to be big enough for you *and* your gear, must be a "natural" shelter in that it fits into the surrounding cityscape, and should be of low interest or usage to its owners.

There are exceptions to the above ground rules, as there are to any set of rules. But if you can see the necessity behind each of the six suggestions, you'll be able to find how each can be mutated to fit the situation. The only rule you cannot break is: be wily. Remember that it is the hunter who thinks he's learned all about tigers who becomes lunch. Cities are dangerous places, particularly for the stranger, who has no walls around him. Be courteous and soft in your dealings with city people, but make your shelter in a safe place.

Here follow some classes of short camp you can find in the city.

Short Camps

The most natural shelter in the city is a house or an apartment. Unfortunately, these cannot be rented for a night at reasonable rates. The two options, then, are to use abandoned ones or to get permission to use others free. Abandoned houses or apartments in the city are very bad news. They are almost always inhabited by people you wouldn't want your sister to marry, and because of this are frequently patrolled by both the police and gangs of uglies. The other option works well.

In most cities there will be an apartment complex under construction. These sites all have — by law — a watchman, drinking water, and a toilet. If you approach the watchman after the workday and ask permission to throw out your roll in one of the unfinished apartments, emphasizing that you'll be gone before the workday starts, you will most times be given permission. This gives you not only a fine shelter — you can sometimes catch places with the carpeting already laid, functional plumbing, etc. — but a person to watch your bike and gear all night.

The next most natural shelter is a garage. There are two types to consider. First is the commercial garage, the indoor parking lot. These have the same advantages as an apartment complex under construction — toilets, water, and a watchman. It is seldom possible to camp free here, but a dollar bill will usually do as rent. You ask the attendant for an unused corner, which you'll always find, or a car space on which your dollar can be considered rent. Your best bet in indoor commercial garages is the multistory place, since these will have quieter corners on the upper floors and the attendants will be more inclined to accept your proposal of cheap rent for the night.

The private garage can most often be found in the suburbs and the use of it can most often be acquired in shopping centers. You approach a man who seems to be the family type — therefore most likely to own a garage — and explain your situation. Use all the techniques for dealing with city folk and add a dash of charm. I've found that on the average, the fourth family man you hit on will have enough envy or curiosity about you to lend you his garage for the night.

Don't approach a woman because most married men take a dim view of their wives bringing home exotic men for the night.

Public buildings, warehouses, and railroad yards are poor bets. They all have strict rules about overnight guests and the enforcement of the rules is usually thorough. The days when you could camp in or around freight yards are long since gone. It is often possible in smaller cities, however, to spend the night as the guest of the police, either in a cell or on the station grounds. I have had about 20 percent success when I've asked to stay overnight in an unused cell and nearly 65 percent success in being allowed to camp on the back edge of the parking lot, a corner of the police garage, or some unused grass between sidewalk and building. The only problem with this kind of camp is the high traffic, complete with lights and noise. Don't consider this unless you are a sound sleeper.

The most available shelter in the city, and with some practice on your part the most efficient, is not buildings at all but containers.

In the industrial portions of any city, along waterfronts, loading and unloading sections, etc., there will be any number of large packing crates and shipping containers. These range from cardboard boxes to standard-sized steel seacrates. It is among these that the nomad will find his best short-camp shelter. The advantages are that no one is likely to think of a stored or discarded box as a motel room, that these things can be found in any city, and that there is little chance that the owner will be around at two A.M. to throw you out.

When using this sort of camp, pick it during the day. Look it over carefully for suitability, for previous inhabitants, for likelihood of current usage by the owner, and for its location. This last is important because you will not often find this sort of shelter in an area where your mount is safe if left outside for a night. You must therefore find a camp within walking distance of a safe parking place or one large enough to shelter your bike, too.

I do not often resort to this sort of camp. Indeed, I do not often camp in the city. But when I do, and use a "found" camp like this, I frequently just stack myself and Ganesh against the side of a disreputable building and throw a large piece of cardboard or something over the both of us, disguising myself as a pile of trash! This not only avoids the question of ownership of the "tent" but means I have to unpack only my sleeping gear.

However, found camps in the city are always risky and at best involve seeking permission to do something quasi-legal or uncomfortable. Most of the time you will have to pay for your camp.

If You Have to Pay

If you are in the city for the night and there is no designated campground within reach; if it's too late or too dark to look for a packing-crate tent; if you can't find a friendly face that looks like it owns a garage; if the bike shops are all closed; if the local constabulary looks like it would rather cut your hair than offer you a cell bunk for the night, then you'll have to pay for a place to lay your head. This is one of the best arguments against cities that I know of.

You have some options and some considerations.

The best place for an overnight camp, if you have to pay for it, is a motel. Motels are cheaper than hotels, and today are more plentiful. Look for one toward the edge of town *off* the main road. Look for an individually owned business rather than a chain. This place will be cheaper than the centrally located chain business, often by a considerable amount. I once found a range of from $32 down to $4.50 within a mile on the same highway, and both within sight of downtown Dallas.

Remember that a motel needs *only* (a) a door that locks, (b) a bed, and (c) water. Anything else is superfluous and you will be paying for things you don't need. You want that lockable door so that you can bring your gear in, and your mount, too, if the door's wide enough.

You can usually find a motel that will fill the above requirements and still be a decent place. A good way to tell in advance is to look for membership notices on the place's billboard. Does it belong to a rating organization you recognize? Does it have anybody's seal of approval? These things will nearly always guarantee that the plumbing works and the room is free of crawlie visitors.

Put no faith in signs advertising acceptance of credit cards, bank cards, etc. These things tell you only that the motel will take money in any form, not what it gives in return.

Long Camps

What if you're in town for a month stopping off to see all the sights? You can't depend on your packing crate being empty every night for a month, nor on that construction site still being available. What do you do for shelter?

Rent a place, of course. But not the sort of place you'd rent if you were not a nomad. To begin with, you have your own furniture — your bed and kitchen, your tools and toys. You need only shelter. This allows you to shop for the least expensive place in the city. Do not worry about neighborhood unless you fear getting your throat cut. With what you save in rent you can buy substantial locks for your room or apartment.

Since you are staying only that month or two and not investing your future in the place, you can scrounge such furniture and fixtures as you desire to supplement your traveling gear. I've found that a sitting surface and an eating/working surface are good things to have in a wooden tent. These can be found or built right off the streets at zero cost.

You look — again — only for a safe place to keep your mount while you are not with it. Remember the definition of shelter and do not pay for more than you need.

Two Raccoons, an old man who lives in a mud hut near South Lake Tahoe, California, says that the white man's tents are designed for bad health. They not only shut out the sun and the air, which heal and carry off illness, but they are filled with things that the person inside doesn't need. This is bad, says Two Raccoons, because everything a man puts in his tent comes to own a little of him, and if he puts too much around him he will no longer have a piece of himself to call his own.

In the long run, I have found this to be quite accurate. Keep that in mind when sheltering in the cities.

20. PLAYING IN THE STREETS

Whatever your choice in city shelters, you'll have to ride in from the country to get to them, which means that you'll be riding in the city. This short chapter covers the special problems of city riding.

Coming In

Entering a city is nearly as dangerous as driving in one. You will be changing riding patterns radically when you come into town, often under adverse circumstances. You will move from high to low speed, from open highway to constricted street, from gentle curve to right-angle turn, from one directional traffic flow to many, and from personal relaxation to tension. Any or all of these conditions can prove dangerous to you if improperly handled.

Let's come into a medium-sized town a step at a time.

First, you will be asked to reduce speed. Note that this is done in stages, going from the 60 or 65 mph on the open road to 45 mph, then down to 35 mph, then possibly down to 25 mph in the seriously congested areas.

Why is it done this way? Why not just post the 25 mph limit immediately?

Because people who've been driving the open road have

altered judgment and reflexes. They react more slowly and their reactions are usually less fine than normal. This is due to the soporific effect of changeless, sustained running. After several hours of constant drone, making only small correctional maneuvers and holding a consistent speed, it takes your brain a while to readjust to the faster demands of city driving. It also takes the muscles longer to react. This gradual adjustment in speed limits upon entering most cities is designed to give your brain and body time to prepare for the demands of in-city driving.

Since you are mounted on an unstable machine that is probably loaded to its capacity, your reactions — good and bad — will have more effect on your safety than an automobilist's or a trucker's. Where the car driver can correct a too-slow turn by whipping the wheel around and screeching through that corner, you will wind up on the pavement if you try an abrupt change of course. Where an emergency stop to correct a too-slow judgment means smoking tires and noise for a trucker, it usually means the pavement again for a biker.

When you come into a city you will face one of two changes in status: speed-limit decreases or heavy increase in traffic. In either case, the instant you are aware of either, put yourself through a wake-up drill. Start by saying *Wake Up! Wake Up!* loudly. Yell it, if you want. This will key a whole range of biological responses in your body, all of which will benefit you.

Next, wake your hands and feet up. Take one hand at a time off the controls and flex the fingers rapidly. Shake the hand vigorously. Make a fist, rotate the arm and shoulder.

Lift your feet and rotate the ankles. Wiggle your toes. Flex your calves and thighs.

Then shift your body and relax your back. Lean well forward between the handlebars and arch your back a couple of times, rotating your neck. Move back and forth on the saddle a couple of times, shifting around to find where the numb spots are.

Finally, massage the back of your neck with one hand and rub your nose. By this time you will have restored circulation to your body, found a couple of aches and numb spots — which will both keep you alert and tell you how badly you need to stop — and dragged your brain into perspective.

If you come in on the surface streets, as you will in smaller towns, be especially watchful for local traffic lunging onto the road. The outskirts of cities harbor all of the motels, quickie restaurants, and saloons, the patrons of which will sail blithely into the street unaware of just how tired and fuzzy you are. Besides, you're only a biker.

Watch also for the Bewildered Tourist, who will meander over all lanes looking for a restaurant that will suit the wife and kids as well as his wallet. These folk are prone to shift lanes all the way across the highway with no notice to anyone.

Watch also for the officer with the ticket book who lurks in wait for the guy who's pushing through the town in a hurry. Said officer often has a thing about motorcyclists.

If you are unsure of routing through the city, pull over and inquire. Do not plow blindly through a strange city's traffic peering for Route 80 signs unless you want to get smeared.

If you come in on a freeway, as you will in the larger cities, stay in the slowest possible lane consistent with your route. You do this because it gives you more time to make and implement decisions, because it keeps you out of the lanes frequented by the hurry-hurry types and the drunks, and because it will cater more readily to your highway-slowed reflexes. Note that I specified the slowest lane consistent with your route. In many freeway systems, the "slow" or exit lane is fine unless you are following the Interstate 10 signs (or whatever) and that portion of the freeway happens to bend off to the left. You will then — if you're in the exit lane — have to cross *all* the lanes in your freeway artery, including the fast ones, to reach the I-10 artery. This is roughly the same as trying to get across the field at the 50-yard line during a punt return in the Superbowl — and about as safe.

Most off ramps "bleed" diagonally into the traffic on the surface. If there is anyone ahead of you on the ramp, watch for a sudden change of mind on that driver's part at the bottom of the ramp. He may cruise smoothly into the traffic pattern, and then again he may get halfway into the lane and jam on his brakes — which leaves you leaned over and coming down on him at anywhere from 15 to 30 mph. Unhealthy at any time.

Entering a city is dangerous and you should be at your most alert, because you will be tired, slow, and mistake-prone, and your most alert will probably just barely get you by if you have an emergency.

On the Streets

Once on the city streets, you will face some odd situations.

I have already covered some of the problems of city riding in Chapters Thirteen and Fourteen, in particular those dealing with power losses and mechanical failures. There are other practical problems that the nomad will face.

You will find that in most cities, a parked touring bike will become the center of a crowd of curious people almost instantly. This is good for striking up conversations but places some strain on you if you have to leave the machine. The problem here is less one of potential theft than of danger to the onlookers. Few of them realize the weight of a packed mount, nor the ease with which it can be pulled over on the young boy who'll try to get into the saddle the minute your eye is diverted. And if that child is injured, guess whose fault it will be?

Parking presents other problems. For instance, many places you'll wish to stop will be on sloping streets. How do you park a bike on a surface that slants at 28 degrees? I once came upon Pine Street, in San Francisco, quite suddenly and from the top. I jammed on Ganesh's brakes and peered straight down my forks at the bay, far, far below. For just an instant it seemed perfectly logical to dismount, throw the bike down the hill, and climb down after it. Yet a day or so later I was confidently parking on the side of that same fearful incline.

A loaded bike has a high center of gravity and will tip over readily on a steep incline. You can't use the center stand on a such a grade because you'd have to push the bike forward — straight uphill — to get off, then hold it back against gravity with your trembling legs. You can't use the side stand unless you can lean the bike to the uphill side of the grade, which sometimes means nosing the bike into the curb, which is illegal in many cities.

The solution in almost all cases is to angle-park the machine with the rear tire on the curb and the "lean" uphill. This position minimizes the actual degree of tilt from the vertical you'll have to deal with, gives you control against the bike running away since the wheel is on the curb, and is legally acceptable most everywhere. The disadvantage is that you'll have to find a parking place on the correct side of the street.

When parking in a metered space, park in the center just as though you were in an auto. If you park near either end of the space, someone with a teeny car will invariably try to share the space with you. Nine times out of ten he will knock your bike over and leave. The tenth time a policeman will come along and give *you* a ticket, not the auto. There are no exceptions to that rule that I know of.

The only place you can park a nomadic bike without having 90 people crawling over it is in a gas station. There will be onlookers but, as a general rule, no touchers. I don't know why this is so but it holds true for me and for the riders I've queried about it.

When you park to eat, to do laundry, or to shop, the rule is: park where you can see the bike and be where you can get to it in a hurry. That is, if you are in a restaurant, park the bike near the front door and sit close to the door yourself. Keep as little distance between you and your mount as you can. This is more to avoid injury lawsuits than theft. If you can't be with the bike, leave someone with it. When I travel with a companion, I stay with Ganesh when she powders her nose, and she stays with him when I powder mine. When we shop, one of us goes in the store and the other plays dashing nomad for the peanut gallery. It's not only good nomadic practice to do this but good public relations. If we're looking for a friend to help me muscle something up a set of stairs, the lady stays with the bike and attracts men. If we're looking for a friend to help the lady do brain surgery or something, I stay with Ganesh and smile a lot.

The other part of being on the streets is the actual riding.

Steel Elephants: Rules for City Riding

Throughout this book I have emphasized how radically different a loaded bike handles. Every aspect of your mount's behavior worsens when you strap your portable home aboard. The only place loading a bike helps is in acquiring high-speed stability, and you are not likely to do much high-speed running in the middle of Salt Lake City.

Your mount will handle its worst when you're in the city. Low-speed maneuvering through herds of traffic will be the hardest form of driving you will experience. Your mount will be sluggish, top-heavy, unsure of itself when cornering, and lacking in both braking and acceleration.

It will be up to you to counter these conditions.

When riding the city streets, remember that you are in the statistically proven most dangerous place on earth. You are on an open plain of concrete, lurching around like a steel elephant, with hunters coming at you from front, back, and both sides, all intent on making messy spots out of you. Remember that you are less visible than other animals on the plain, and that you are less important to most of those others than their fellow beasts. Remember that you are a set of quick reflexes — yourself — coupled to a slow response — your mount. Think of yourself as a very fat man at a dance and strive to be graceful.

Apply all the rules of good riding you know and give each an extra measure of caution. Make all your time and distance margins larger. A good rule of thumb is to figure turns and stopping distances as though you were rainriding. If it happens that you *are* rainriding, allow a 30 percent margin on everything, over and above your bad-weather allowances. To the passing herd this will make you look like somebody's cautious aunt, but it will keep you alive.

The rules for city riding are:

Signal clearly and twice. If you're turning left, put on your turn indicators *and* stick your hand out.

Look before making any change of speed or direction.

Keep a zone of empty space around you — a large one.

Move deliberately, never on impulse.

Give way, whatever the situation.

These are basic, common-sense rules that will give you a survival attitude and will keep you, your mount, and your gear together as a happy little group. Coupled with what you know about shelter in the city, you are pretty well equipped to get around.

Now, let's look at how you can feed yourself and your mount while a stranger in the town.

21. THE MARKETPLACE

Money is the nomad's best tool. It is mutable into any shape needed, it is portable, lightweight, and proof against wind and water. The only problem seems to be getting enough of it. This problem is especially acute for the two-wheel traveler because he is forever in an unknown market, and he has limited ability to carry trade-goods or tools with him. In this chapter we'll look at money and how you get it while on the road.

Money as Energy Flow

Money is a form of frozen energy. It is unlocked — thawed — into whatever shape you need to replace a given kind of energy you have expended. It buys food to replace bodily energy, labor to replace work energy, beauty to replace esthetic energy. The thing to note about money, then, is that it is a symbolic substance. It symbolizes those things that it will buy and has little intrinsic value in and of itself. It is merely a catalyst in the flow of energy from form to form and point to point. It is a very nomadic material.

The importance of this view of money lies in the concept of energy flow and what that implies. The implication being that if you can find alternate catalysts to start the flow, you don't need money. The whole concept of swap meets, bartering, and value exchange proves that other catalysts not only exist but are active in the modern world.

As a two-wheel nomad you will be concerned with money at some point in your journeys, even if you have sufficient reserves for a long trip. The first approach you need make to the subject is interpreting your needs in terms of energy instead of dollars. That is, decide what you want money for. Food? Shelter? Repairs for your mount?

Next, consider how you can avoid the intermediate and symbolic step called "money." Can you find what you desire free? Can it be traded for? Worked for? Bargained for? Bear in mind that the less malleable a tool is, the easier it is to find free or cheap. The energy tool called "food" is more readily available for the asking than the versatile tool called "cash." You can find a shelter by asking around the shopping center's parking lot much more easily than you can find $10 for a motel room.

Keep in mind that the thing you are interested in is the flow of energy, and that you seek the path of least resistance. You look for a favorable trade of low-versatility energy (fixing the lady's screen door) for high-versatility energy (a good meal). The order of priorities for energy trades is: Work for it, barter for it, buy it.

The reasoning is that it is easier to replenish work energy than a trade item or cash.

All forms of money flow you will undertake fall in one of the three categories above. In each there will be overlapping. You will occasionally trade money for labor, labor for food, work for money, trade-goods for shelter, etc.

Let us look at some forms of energy acquisition.

Why There Are No Odd Jobs

The most common myth among beginning travelers is that a person can still make his way on the odd job or found opportunity. The saddest stories on the road belong to the novice nomad who finds himself or herself broke and hungry and far from home, completely shattered that there are no jobs picking fruit or tending bar. After all, Dylan and Guthrie and Belafonte all sang about the glories of migrant labor, right? And Baez, too!

But most of us listen only to the parts about working in the fresh air and sunshine. We don't listen to the part about twelve-hour days of backbreaking labor for an average of 46¢ an hour.

There are two reasons why there are no odd jobs anymore. One is efficiency and the other is the law of supply and demand. The efficiency comes in the form of unions, labor pools, mechanization, and all the myriad methods businesses use to cut costs. There are few carrot-pulling jobs in the Imperial Valley today because there are huge machines that pull faster and better than human hands.

The second factor — supply and demand — is more prevalent in the cities. The supply in this case being nomadic labor and the demand being available jobs. As far back as 1946, when millions of men came home from the wars to find their jobs gone, the number of drifting laborers outreached the number of casual jobs. Since then, despite an ever-spiraling growth rate in business, the situation has been unchanged. This is especially true in picturesque, resort, and high-energy cities, where the summer tide of travelers has become a flood.

A third factor enters here, the Iron Wage Law. This is a dictum that states, "The going wage for a job is the least someone will do it for." If you try to get your cesspool cleaned out in a town full of executives, you'll pay dearly for the labor. But if you're in a town full of half-starved migrants . . .

In sum, there are fewer and fewer casual jobs to be found in the rural areas, and there is an increasingly bad supply-demand ratio in the cities. For the unskilled or untrained person, making a living at the odd job is out of the question.

How to Find an Odd Job Anyway

Still, casual jobs are there, and *somebody* gets each one. Here's how to be that someone.

There are four things to do when trying for an odd job:

One: concentrate on jobs you can actually do. There's a tendency in all of us to develop imaginary skills when we get hungry, and for those skills to grow in direct proportion to our hunger. I have been known to be a master bartender, deep-sea diver, and trainer of wild cats on command — as long as the only proof I had to offer was my own glowing description of my capabilities. The problem is that nobody pays for words, only action, and the wages you'll get for that hour's labor you do before the boss discovers your incompetence won't pay for the time you've invested in pulling the wool over his eyes.

If you cannot actually wash windows, don't say you can. Either tell the truth and hope your honest face will win you the job over more experienced competition or move on to another job.

Two: be there first. The majority of casual jobs go to the first qualified person available to fill them. To a person who is hiring quick labor, all laborers look alike. This is especially important in labor-pool situations, such as day-labor hiring halls, dock work, and crop tending.

Three: come dressed for work. This is the most overlooked aspect of casual job-hunting, and the one that most often wins or loses a job. You should not expect to be hired to wait tables in a restaurant if you apply for the job in cowboy boots and a T-shirt, nor to unload trucks if you arrive in a suit.

The question of dress — or image, if you will — is more precise than I've indicated above. A loading-crew boss will look not simply for work shoes but for steel-toed shoes, and worn ones at that. A man hiring a tack welder will look for weld-metal burns on the applicant's jeans. He'll look for a worn spot in one of the rear pockets; that's where a welder carries his rods. He'll look for a pair of gloves — and don't tell him you don't use gloves unless you've got the scars on your hands to prove it!

This is not usually a conscious process on an employer's part. He seldom goes through a visual inspection as though it were a "thing." But it is there nonetheless and will be the major factor in determining where that employer's eye first stops when all of you would-be tack welders step out of the throng in answer to his call. Remember, look like a pro in whatever job you are applying for.

Four: stand out in some fashion. Do or wear or be something that will attract the employer's eye and cause you to stick in his memory. If you're after some hard-hat job where everyone is wearing jeans and work shirts, throw a bright bandanna around your neck or wear a silly hat. I used to wear a raggedy straw hat with a loud yellow plastic flower bobbing on top.

The trick is in keeping your attention-getter subdued enough not to scare the employer off, yet obvious enough to catch his eye. The secret here is: keep it simple and small. A lady nomad I know takes casual work as a cashier in towns she passes through. She has an easy trick: being a pretty girl, she wears a pair of unflattering eyeglasses — which she doesn't need. The glasses have a broken temple piece, which she has repaired with a strip of *bright red* tape. The tape is small, but it draws the eye and stays in the memory. Once my friend has established that piece of tape in her potential employer's mind, she removes the glasses and shakes out her hair. This usually paralyzes her target, if it's male, and still gives her an edge with women employers.

A mannerism will often do as well, provided it doesn't offend the employer. I once applied for a Christmas season's work behind a counter in a large store. I found that I looked just like the other thirty supplicants — all in suits and ties. When my interview came, I noticed that the personnel man had a small moustache. All through the interview I made a point of absentmindedly twirling the ends of my own, so that I soon had a fine curl on either side of my nose. When I left, I not only had the job but the personnel manager's compliments — somewhat envious — on my cookieduster.

Of course, you don't comb your hair when being interviewed by a bald man.

The odd-job rules, then, are: know the work, be there first, look the part, and be an individual. This won't guarantee you the job but it will tilt the table a little in your favor.

Casual labor is a precarious living at best, and not too rewarding even to the persistent. There are, however, many other approaches to money.

Portable Skills

One of the best approaches is to have a portable skill.

As used here, "skill" means any form of energy flow you possess that will bring in better money than casual labor. In other words, while bartending is definitely a skill, and definitely portable, it comes under casual labor because of the low income it usually produces and because bartending doesn't require formal training. Being a practical nurse or a draftsman, on the other hand, counts as having a portable skill, since these jobs are not open to the labor pool and produce a respectable income.

The other factor to consider in having a portable skill is the market for it. It's well and good to be the best-qualified paleoanthropologist in the Western Hemisphere, but how many cities will have work for you?

In the main, the best portable skills to own are those used in the construction trades, the maintenance trades, the teaching professions, and sales. I've mentioned welding several times in this book — with good reason. A proficient welder can get a job in any city, any time of the year, and make a minimum of $2 or $3 an hour. Even if no welders' jobs are available, he can usually hire on as a welder's helper at enough money to eat quite well. The same holds true for electricians, plumbers, carpenters, bricklayers, carpet layers, cement finishers, etc.

In the professions, teachers can tutor or substitute, salesmen with any degree of skill can work anywhere, anytime, and managerial talent never goes unappreciated.

When considering a portable skill, check the help-wanted columns in the paper. Get several out-of-town papers and do the same. Look for (1) the kind of skilled jobs most often advertised, and (2) jobs you are peculiarly qualified for. The first category will give you an idea of what to train for, and the second what sort of market there is for any specialty you might have.

Remember that as a nomad, you are essentially casual or short-term labor to your employers, just as if you were in a day-labor pool. Don't ever lie to an employer about how long you expect to remain. The world is a lot smaller than you'd think, and the word will get around your section of the job market sooner or later that you're one who leaves the boss hanging.

By far the best, most dependable, and most interesting way to make money on the road is to develop a talent.

The Crafty Trader

Throughout history, the nomad has survived by murder, theft, and trade, in about that order. Today, governments and corporations have taken the first two options from us, but the third remains. In this area the nomad has been — and still is — supreme. He has all the advantages. He hasn't the overhead that the shop owner faces, nor the taxes. He is not dependent on the market that passes his door, since he goes to the market. He doesn't have to spend fortunes on advertising, since he trades on a one-to-one basis.

In short, the nomad's natural place on the energy-transference line is as a trader.

But what does he trade?

The product is limited by the mode and the nomad's inclinations. That is, it is difficult to be a rhinoceros salesman if you cannot carry your samples around on a motorcycle or if you don't happen to like rhinoceri. Aside from these two limitations, the field is open to imagination. Here are some points to consider:

Everybody has some sort of marketable talent. I have not, in ten years of looking, found an exception to this. Many people do not believe they have one, but this is usually because they have not tried to find one or because they didn't realize the one they own was salable.

The best talents are those that result in a physical product. Knitting is good, for example, because it results in handbags and sweaters that can be sold for money.

The best products are those with universal markets. Universal means not only "everybody wants one" but "I can sell these anywhere I go." This rules out making snowshoes if you're aiming for Costa Rica.

The most salable products are individual. Make something that is unique or that is uniquely yours. If you are that knitter I mentioned, every handbag you make will not only be Hand Made, but Different, two of the most potent sales aids there are — and you'll be telling the truth!

The best products are those that can be sold one-on-one, or direct. That is, products that you take up to someone and offer to sell to him or her. Sales made through shops are fine if you can get cash for your goods, but this is very seldom the case. Most often, things bought wholesale are taken either on consignment — which means that you get paid only if your stuff sells — or on a delay of from 30 to 90 days. Both systems leave you without either goods or money.

Some of the things people make for money are astounding. Here are a few, just to stimulate your imagination.

Makin' It

Knitting, crocheting, sewing. Possibly the most popular trade among lady nomads, and one of the best there is. The tools and materials are light and compact, available everywhere, and require no care. The most successful woman I know carries two crocheted bags over her shoulder as she wanders around the art museums and city streets. One bag holds yarn, the other finished shawls, caps, and purses. She works as she walks and as soon as she finishes a piece she just stops passing ladies until she either sells the piece or one from her bag. She clears around $3.25 per article and averages about $250 a month at her trade. I know ladies who double that, but they like to work a lot.

Tin art. I know several variations on this, but the best belongs to Willie Wheater, of Bluefield, West Virginia. He makes intricate, delicate candle lanterns from plain old tin cans, cutting patterns in them with an acetylene torch (he carries the torch and rents the bottles locally). He stains the finished product with a secret compound that antiques them and hangs them on poles, trees, or a piece of line beside the highway. He works right beside the road, looking like some sort of weird Martian in his goggles and fuzzy hair, and people stop in droves to buy the lanterns from his wife, Marian. Willie clears about $14 per lantern and can make two a day. He works for a week, then sells for a day or two.

Photography. Jack and Leda carry two fancy Polaroid Land cameras around the city streets and take pictures of office workers, lovers, businessmen, etc. It's an impulse sale, like flowers, and they do it smoothly. They mount the prints in handsome little folders that they have made for them in Baltimore and sell the whole thing for $2. The entire operation from approach to "thank you" runs about three minutes, and the profit margin is about 100 percent, which means that each of them has a potential income of $20 an hour, and that ain't bad money for *anybody*.

Leana makes dolls out of beer bottles. Harvey does pen-and-ink portraits. Two kids I know recite poetry and play the flute for passersby. I know a man who has a watch-repair business honed down to fit on a motorcycle. Another sharpens knives (and averages $4.80 an hour at it).

Peter Martin used to buy light bulbs wholesale and sell them door to door. "Lady" — holding up bulb as she answers the door — "If you don't have a burned-out bulb in your house right now, I'll leave." One of the fastest sales in the business. And at 14¢ wholesale and 49¢ retail, the money is very good.

I know wood-carvers, leatherworkers, silversmiths, soap carvers, puppet makers and furniture refinishers who have made their skills portable and learned to trade them on the street. The list could go on to fill this book, but the above will give you some idea of the breadth possible with a little thought.

Probably the all-time champion nomad's living is made by a fellow named Leonard whom I met on the Mexican border. Leonard ties fishing flies. He has been doing it some time and is quite good. He has a tiny, machine-turned vise in which he clamps the flies, and he ties them while waving his arms around his tent and telling you completely outrageous fishing stories — then pulling out the photographs to prove them. Leonard can tie 12 flies an hour, all day long. He sells them in gas stations, to fishermen in campgrounds, in country stores and supermarkets, and on the streets of the cities. He gets $5 retail and $3 wholesale for the flies. If you care to add that up, you'll get somewhere between $36 and $60 an hour.

Money on the road, energy flow, is a matter of knowing what you want, knowing where to find it, and being prepared for it when you do. The best way to make a living on the road is to have something unique to sell. It is best because it is most direct, and the energy flow — the money — is immediate.

You now have a home and a mount to carry it on, an idea of what it is like to live in the wild and in the city as a nomad, and some suggestions about how to make your way financially. There remains only the final question: why should you consider this sort of uncomfortable, precarious, compacted life in the first place?

Perhaps the next chapter can answer that.

22.

The Persistent Nomad

Nearly a century ago, Yellow-Hair Custer led a crack troop of United States cavalry into a grassy valley near a river called the Little Bighorn. He was looking for an aboriginal tribe-leader named Sitting Bull, and he found him.

About a century ago, Frederic Augustus Thesiger, 2nd Baron Chelmsford, led the finest army in the world across Roarke's Drift to subdue King Cetshwayo's Zulus, and at Isandhlwana he was obliterated.

The last two great nomadic cultures thus made the same mistake at almost the same time: each won a major victory over its civilized opponent. Within two decades, both the Plains Indians of America and the Imperial Zulu nation of Africa had ceased to exist except for broken remnants and scattered individuals.

Both peoples had come to war with pointed sticks and raw courage, facing rifles and Gatling guns. Both had won their victories on blunders by the civilized commanders. And both lost not only their land but their cultural existence. Each was in a race for a continent, with a way of life at stake, and because neither people realized it *was* a race, each lost.

Or did they?

The Zulu nation that Shaka welded together in southern Africa was the high point of civilization as it could be applied then. The Plains tribes of American Indians were the high point of development on this continent. Who remembers the name of three eastern woodland Indians? Who can name the accomplishments of Nasha-Hawtwa? Yet every American child knows who Geronimo is, and Sitting Bull, and Red Cloud, and Little Big Man, and Cochise. And in England, which felt the scarring thrust of the assegais, the names of Cetshwayo and Shaka, Uhamu and Dingane, Mbopa and Mpande, are known to schoolchildren, and regimental rolls hold names like Ulundi, Umfolozi, Blood River, Helpmaakar, Ityotyotsi and Mahlabatini Plain, all washed with English blood spilled by the Zulu. But who remembers the Bantu from whom the Zulu came? Who can name a single Hottentot, driven out by the Bantu? One solitary Bushman, driven out by the Hottentot?

In both cases, on both continents, the high-water mark of the indigenous peoples was reached by nomads. The Indian followed the buffalo, the Zulu his cattle. Neither believed in or utilized fences. When conquest came, it came as it would come to us if the Martians suddenly landed with force fields and death rays; frightening and unstoppable and beyond understanding. The Zulu did not understand the principle of the explosive artillery shell. They reasoned it out as well as they could with the science and technology available to them and concluded that death came from small British soldiers concealed in the shells, who leaped out in the burst of smoke and flame. Consequently, when a shell burst in their midst, warriors rushed into the smoke pall, stabbing with their assegais at the small soldiers they thought were there.

You perhaps smiled at that? Think of the *courage* it would take to charge into something you didn't understand, that killed your friends in a way you'd never seen, and that was never hurt by your attacks.

We have a tendency to believe that those who win are superior. This presupposes both absolute justice and absolute judgment, neither of which is a reality as yet. We are, in fact, beginning to find that out in the modern world. As this is being written, the American Indian is coming again to the forefront of our consciousness, teaching, demanding, asserting. We are beginning to understand that there are other values than ours, and that we may have won only the wars, while losing the peace. History has come around far enough now that the story of the Zulu nation is beginning to be heard, and the "winners" in South Africa are covered with opprobrium for their shameful attempts to sanctify a belief that a man's skin can make him inferior or superior.

Throughout history, it has been the nomadic peoples who have innovated and created. They were the travelers, the traders, the thieves and scoundrels who built every road the sedentary people ever walked. They have been the pollinators of culture, the cross-fertilizers of social systems. The nomad has originated or spread every idea, as far back as man's memory goes.

Of course, the fearful who live behind locks and walls remember only the brutal. They remember the Vikings as the ultimate berserk plunderer — which is true. But they forget that the Vikings provided three-fourths of the kings, administrators, farmers and merchants of Europe and much of Asia for better than 500 years. It's a rare Caucasian who doesn't have Viking blood in him, no matter what part of the world his ancestors came from.

Popular history teaches that the knights of Europe wrested the Holy Land from the infidel, but the truth is that no European flag waved over any part of that land a scant decade after the last Crusade ran out of things to steal. The further truth is that the Flower of Chivalry were uncouth, illiterate thugs who went to steal kingdoms and brought back manners, algebra, astronomy, the Greek writings, and a healthy respect for little men in silk dresses with very sharp swords.

Who has won? There are no more nomadic cultures. The fencemakers and towerbuilders have triumphed in this age and reign supreme. No buffalo roam the plains. No herds of royal kine blanket the veldt of Natal and Zululand. No mile-long caravans set out across the Empty Quarter of the Sahara. And the Romany still look for the Land of the Great Horses.

And in America, the common man lies awake at night, wondering who he is. In Britain, the corpse of a centuries-dead social system putrefies lives and abilities. In France, the world's highest alcoholism rate climbs steadily. In

Japan, a boy murders his own father for the first time in recorded history. In Germany, old men with soulless eyes talk about the good old days when the Jewish Problem almost got settled.

There is a sickness in the world today, and it comes of ignoring basic needs. Man was a nomad for millennia; he's been a city dweller for mere centuries. This is not enough time for evolution to damp the drives with which he lived for so long. There is an urge, a *need* to be moving and among the things of the earth, and we ignore it at our psychic and physical peril.

This urge is a persistent one, and it has enough strength to hold up under the demands of a changing world. The Romany now drive mobile homes instead of horse wagons, but they are Gypsies still. The Eskimo now fishes from a snowmobile, but he still fishes for his living. The Navaho drives a pickup from his hogan to the sheep, but he still sings the old songs to his herd.

Those of us who weren't born into a nomadic heritage are finally on the road, not in spite of technology but *because* of it. With the standardization of jobs, material things, and viewpoints; with transportation and communication facilities both standardized and universal; with enough technology-produced leisure to explore, man is now free to go where he will and as he will. And he need not live the bare-bones existence that was for most of his passage on this planet the only fate he owned. While there are fences around everything, there are also roads through the fences. While the cities blight the landscape in every direction, there is still more landscape than city — and it is likely to remain that way in spite of doom prophets. While the people are more and the green less, there is still a massive balance in favor of the trees. There is much world out there, in spite of man.

The important point to remember is that if a person

carries his home with him he will live less expensively than if he were rooted, thus reducing one of the holds that cities have on him. He will make better judgments, be more capable, and win more competitions for jobs, mates, or whatever if he is a traveler and self-sufficient. Most important, he will be a happier, more peaceful person, for he will have the security of knowing himself and his capabilities firsthand, having tested them.

With all the above in consideration, the question isn't why a person should become a two-wheel nomad, but why should he not?

SOURCES APPENDIX

SOURCES APPENDIX

NOTE: Many items referred to in the text are not listed specifically here, but can be found through one or more sources listed. For example, I've not listed an address for the EZEE trowel I recommended in Chapter Nine because it is available through any camping store, or through most of the publications listed below. Likewise, I've not given an address for Elite Insurance Company, since it can be found in almost any motorcycle magazine.

In general, specific technologies, such as fairings, clothing, or camping gear, are given separate listings, and secondary items, such as tools or insurance, are included in the appropriate high-yield source. Look for motorcycle gear through the bike magazine publishers, and everything else not specifically listed through the general catalogues, such as *The Whole Earth Catalogue.*

HIGH-YIELD SOURCES

Much information in one spot.

The Mother Earth News
Box 38
Madison, Wisconsin 44057

Back-to-the-land hints, products, and publications, and contact with other folks.

The Whole Earth Catalogue
558 Santa Cruz Avenue
Menlo Park, California 94025

The Sears catalogue of the counterculture, the nonculture, and the nomads. Everything you always wanted to know about everything.

Peterson Publishing Company
8490 Sunset Boulevard
Hollywood, California 90069

Publishers of motorcycle magazines. A request gets you a list of publications, the best of which is *Motorcyclist*. Bike and accessory info.

Nationwide Publishing
Box 8617
La Crescenta, California 91214

Same as above.

Road Rider
Box 678
South Laguna, California 92677

The only magazine devoted to the two-wheel nomad. *The* source of high-yield nomad info.

Bagnell Publishing Company
Box 507
Lake Arrowhead, California 92352

Bike books, including *Two-Wheel Camping and Touring.*

SOURCES: FAIRINGS

Bates Industries
701 Cowles Street
Long Beach, California 90801

Butler & Smith
Walnut Street and Hudson Avenue
Norwood, New Jersey 07648

Califia Industries, Inc.
1015 East Elm Avenue
Fullerton, California 92631

Clinton Sport Sales
Box 417, R.D. 1
Freeport, Pennsylvania 16229

Fibre-Mold
5315 East Admiral Place
Tulsa, Oklahoma 74115

Wixom Brothers
1637 East Burnett
Long Beach, California 90806

Vetter Fairings
Box 927
Rantoul, Illinois 61866

SOURCES: CAMPING AND NOMADIC GEAR

Clothing

Bates Industries
701 Cowles Street
Long Beach, California 90801

Top Gear
80 Pompton Avenue
Verona, New Jersey 07044

Herm's Leathertogs
701 Northhampton Street
Easton, Pennsylvania 18042

Wheels of Man
First Federal Building
208 East Wisconsin Avenue
Milwaukee, Wisconsin 53202

Hap Jones Distributing Company
Box 3068
San Francisco, California

J. Barbour & Sons, Ltd.
Simonside, South Shields
County Durham
England

Lewis, Ltd.
124 Great Portland Street
London, WIA2DL
England

Some of the above carry many things but I've listed them primarily for their weatherskins.

General gear

Bishop's Ultimate Outdoor Equipment
6804 Millwood Road
Bethesda, Maryland 20034

Thomas Black & Sons, Inc.
930 Ford Street
Ogdensburg, New York 13669

Sierra Designs
4th and Addison Streets
Berkeley, California 94710

Eureka Tent and Awning
625 Conklin Road
Binghamton, New York 13902

Gerry
5450 North Valley Highway
Denver, Colorado 80216

Stephenson's
23206 Hatteras Street
Woodland Hills, California 91364

Great Outdoors Camping
4421 Hollister
Santa Barbara, California 93110

Alpine Designs
6185 East Arapahoe Street
Box 3561
Boulder, Colorado 80303

Frostline Outdoor Equipment
Box 2190
Boulder, Colorado 80303

Eastern Mountain Sports, Inc.
1041 Commonwealth Avenue
Boston, Massachusetts 02215

The North Face
308 Columbus Avenue
San Francisco, California 94133

Holubar
Box 7
Boulder, Colorado 80303

Antarctic Products, Ltd.
Box 223
Nelson, New Zealand

The above sources will give you both specifics and direction for further research, should you need any. Here follow a couple of good books, places, and people you should know about.

BOOKS

The Complete Walker, a trip through the head of Colin Fletcher, who is the backpacker's backpacker. What it's like to get your head into walking. From *Whole Earth, The Mother Earth News,* or any bookstore. It costs $7.95.

Let's Try Barter, the only book I know of on the many ways a nomad can avoid using money. Many useful tips. By Charles Morrow and available from *T.M.E.N.*

Stalking the Wild Asparagus, the first—and most useful—of Euell Gibbons's books on how to eat your way across the backyard stone-free. Costs $2.95 in paperback. From *W.E.C.*, *T.M.E.N.*, or the bookstore.

Being Your Own Wilderness Doctor, by Bradford Angier and Russ Kodet. An emergency fix-your-own-tumor book. Tells you what a doctor would do, in language you can follow. $3.95.

PLACES

Rising Fawn, Georgia. Just south of Chattanooga, Tennessee. A mountaintop campground right out of those American Romantic paintings of the Hudson Valley School. You expect Natty Bumppo to step around the corner any moment.

Horse Pens 40, south of Steele, Alabama. A miles-long natural cathedral of rock and silence run by a family named Musgrove who bought the land to keep the developers out. Folk-arts festivals every October.

North Truro Campground, right out on the tip of Cape Cod, Massachusetts. A commercial ground set in pine trees and sand dunes, a few miles from Provincetown. Summers it becomes an international community of peaceful sun and water freaks.

Del Rio, Texas, the whole area is campable, with the Amistad National Recreation Area topping the desirable list. Open plain, huge lake over sunken towns, and lots of sun.

Hungry Mother State Park, near Marion, Virginia, is a fine example of the large, well-run state park. Set in beautiful hills, with a magnificent lake, it's one of my favorite places in this country.

PEOPLE

Anybody at John Penton's BMW dealership, outside Cleveland, Ohio, is a worthwhile talking-trip. John holds many long-distance riding records and is the designer and builder of Penton motorcycles. This is the cleanest, best-run dealership in the United States.

If you're in Los Angeles, look up Peter at Phantom Motorcycles. Pete has a sign on the wall that reads, "If it's English, American or Stolen, just truck it on out of here."

Aside from that small prejudice, Pete runs the best People's Repair Service I know of. He's my BMW mechanic. Honest work at honest prices.

Dennis Frey dropped out of aerospace to open Great Outdoors Camping in Santa Barbara. He smokes a foul pipe, talks a mile a minute, and once drove all the way to Los Angeles to get a sleeping bag to me the night before a trip. He has the best shopful of bike nomads' equipment there is, since he does his camping off an old and very disreputable Honda 450. If you need it, Dennis has it — although he'll probably talk you into something cheaper and better.

Acknowledgments

Special appreciation goes to the following friends:
Bill Phillips, gentleman and scholar.
Mike Hamilburg, patient man.
Dennis Frey, who listens well.
Jim Miller, a long-distance friend.
Augutendarssak, of Umalak, Greenland.
Stalking Bird, Pear Tree, Horse's Eye, and
Butchers Slowly, my brothers.

And, of course, the ladies, who are not enumerated
because each was special.

CHECKLISTS

INSPECTION SEQUENCE

EACH MORNING

1. *Tires.* Correct pressure. Rims seated and free of dirt. Treads free of stones and cuts.
2. *Wheels.* Spokes tight. Axle nut tight. No leakage from hubs. Brake linkages tight.
3. *Drive.* Chain tensioned correctly. Chain oiled and free of dirt. (Shaft drives, check oil level at rear axle.)
4. *Systems.* Check levels of gas, oil, and water. Check engine dipstick for quality of oil (grit? water? burned?).
5. *Controls.* Cables adjusted. Lever linkages adjusted. Switches operating. Lights and horn operating. Mirrors adjusted correctly.
6. *Frame.* Tighten nuts and bolts. Check swing arm for wear. Check front end for wobble.
7. *Load.* Check for windloading, weatherpacking, and weight distribution. Inspect your side storage system for rips, tears, or breaks. Test your bunji cords for wear and flexibility.

EACH BREAK

1. *Run* procedures 1, 2, 3, 4, and 7, with particular attention to your brake cables, tires, and load.

TRIP SHEETS

	GAS	OIL	FOOD	REPAIRS	
DAY 1.					
2.					
3.					
4.					
5.					
6.					
7.					
8.					
9.					
10.					
11.					
12.					
13.					
14.					
15.					
16.					
17.					
18.					
19.					
20.					
21.					
22.					
23.					
24.					

	CAMP FEES	TOTAL COSTS	MILEAGE		
			START	END	TOTAL

	GAS	OIL	FOOD	REPAIRS	
DAY 1.					
2.					
3.					
4.					
5.					
6.					
7.					
8.					
9.					
10.					
11.					
12.					
13.					
14.					
15.					
16.					
17.					
18.					
19.					
20.					
21.					
22.					
23.					
24.					

	CAMP FEES	TOTAL COSTS	MILEAGE		
			START	END	TOTAL

	GAS	OIL	FOOD	REPAIRS	
DAY 1.					
2.					
3.					
4.					
5.					
6.					
7.					
8.					
9.					
10.					
11.					
12.					
13.					
14.					
15.					
16.					
17.					
18.					
19.					
20.					
21.					
22.					
23.					
24.					

	CAMP FEES	TOTAL COSTS	MILEAGE		
			START	END	TOTAL

TRIP SHEETS

	GAS	OIL	FOOD	REPAIRS	
DAY 1.					
2.					
3.					
4.					
5.					
6.					
7.					
8.					
9.					
10.					
11.					
12.					
13.					
14.					
15.					
16.					
17.					
18.					
19.					
20.					
21.					
22.					
23.					
24.					

	CAMP FEES	TOTAL COSTS	MILEAGE		
			START	END	TOTAL

TRIP SHEETS

	GAS	OIL	FOOD	REPAIRS	
DAY 1.					
2.					
3.					
4.					
5.					
6.					
7.					
8.					
9.					
10.					
11.					
12.					
13.					
14.					
15.					
16.					
17.					
18.					
19.					
20.					
21.					
22.					
23.					
24.					

	CAMP FEES	TOTAL COSTS	MILEAGE		
			START	END	TOTAL

	GAS	OIL	FOOD	REPAIRS	
DAY 1.					
2.					
3.					
4.					
5.					
6.					
7.					
8.					
9.					
10.					
11.					
12.					
13.					
14.					
15.					
16.					
17.					
18.					
19.					
20.					
21.					
22.					
23.					
24.					

	CAMP FEES	TOTAL COSTS	MILEAGE		
			START	END	TOTAL

CAMPGROUND DIRECTORY

Date Arrived Date Departed

Name of Campground

Type of Campground

Location of Campground

FACILITIES

RATING: *Excellent Good Fair Poor*

Tent Site

Toilets/Washhouse

Laundry

Grocery

Staff

Cost

Scenery

Reaction to Motorcyclist

Weather

Comments

OVERALL RATING

CAMPGROUND DIRECTORY

Date Arrived Date Departed

Name of Campground

Type of Campground

Location of Campground

FACILITIES

RATING: *Excellent* *Good* *Fair* *Poor*

Tent Site

Toilets/Washhouse

Laundry

Grocery

Staff

Cost

Scenery

Reaction to Motorcyclist

Weather

Comments

OVERALL RATING

CAMPGROUND DIRECTORY

Date Arrived Date Departed

Name of Campground

Type of Campground

Location of Campground

FACILITIES

RATING: *Excellent* *Good* *Fair* *Poor*

Tent Site

Toilets/Washhouse

Laundry

Grocery

Staff

Cost

Scenery

Reaction to Motorcyclist

Weather

Comments

OVERALL RATING

CAMPGROUND DIRECTORY

Date Arrived Date Departed

Name of Campground

Type of Campground

Location of Campground

FACILITIES

RATING: *Excellent Good Fair Poor*

Tent Site

Toilets/Washhouse

Laundry

Grocery

Staff

Cost

Scenery

Reaction to Motorcyclist

Weather

Comments

OVERALL RATING

CAMPGROUND DIRECTORY

Date Arrived   Date Departed

Name of Campground

Type of Campground

Location of Campground

FACILITIES

RATING: *Excellent* *Good* *Fair* *Poor*

Tent Site

Toilets/Washhouse

Laundry

Grocery

Staff

Cost

Scenery

Reaction to Motorcyclist

Weather

Comments

OVERALL RATING

CAMPGROUND DIRECTORY

Date Arrived Date Departed

Name of Campground

Type of Campground

Location of Campground

FACILITIES

RATING: *Excellent Good Fair Poor*

Tent Site

Toilets/Washhouse

Laundry

Grocery

Staff

Cost

Scenery

Reaction to Motorcyclist

Weather

Comments

OVERALL RATING

CAMPGROUND DIRECTORY

Date Arrived Date Departed

Name of Campground

Type of Campground

Location of Campground

FACILITIES

RATING: *Excellent Good Fair Poor*

Tent Site

Toilets/Washhouse

Laundry

Grocery

Staff

Cost

Scenery

Reaction to Motorcyclist

Weather

Comments

OVERALL RATING

CAMPGROUND DIRECTORY

Date Arrived Date Departed

Name of Campground

Type of Campground

Location of Campground

FACILITIES

RATING: *Excellent Good Fair Poor*

Tent Site

Toilets/Washhouse

Laundry

Grocery

Staff

Cost

Scenery

Reaction to Motorcyclist

Weather

Comments

OVERALL RATING

CAMPGROUND DIRECTORY

Date Arrived Date Departed

Name of Campground

Type of Campground

Location of Campground

FACILITIES

RATING: *Excellent Good Fair Poor*

Tent Site

Toilets/Washhouse

Laundry

Grocery

Staff

Cost

Scenery

Reaction to Motorcyclist

Weather

Comments

OVERALL RATING

CAMPGROUND DIRECTORY

Date Arrived Date Departed

Name of Campground

Type of Campground

Location of Campground

FACILITIES

RATING: *Excellent* *Good* *Fair* *Poor*

Tent Site

Toilets/Washhouse

Laundry

Grocery

Staff

Cost

Scenery

Reaction to Motorcyclist

Weather

Comments

OVERALL RATING

CAMPGROUND DIRECTORY

Date Arrived Date Departed

Name of Campground

Type of Campground

Location of Campground

FACILITIES

RATING: *Excellent Good Fair Poor*

Tent Site

Toilets/Washhouse

Laundry

Grocery

Staff

Cost

Scenery

Reaction to Motorcyclist

Weather

Comments

OVERALL RATING